D1413238

Roles of Living Things

Theme: Constancy and Change

THINK LIKE A SCIENTIST

THINK LIKE A SCIENTIST

FIND THAT INSECT

Can you find an insect in this photo? If you look carefully, you'll see a wandering leaf nymph. It looks just like one of the plant leaves surrounding it. Animals that are able to blend in with their environment are hidden from their enemies. This leaf nymph can hide from hungry birds that could make a quick meal of it. Blending in with their environment helps animals survive to produce offspring.

THINK LIKE A SCIENTIST

Questioning In this unit you'll study how living things get what they need to live, and how living things change and adapt to their environment. You'll investigate questions such as these.

- How Do Living Things Get the Food They Need?
- How Are Living Things Adapted for Protection?

Observing, Testing, Hypothesizing In the Activity "Blending In," you'll find out how animals hide from their enemies. You'll also hypothesize why it is hard to find insects that blend in with their environment.

Researching In the Resource "Hiding Out and Other Defenses," you'll find out about many ways that plants and animals protect themselves from their enemies.

Drawing Conclusions After you've completed your investigations, you'll draw conclusions about what you've learned— and get new ideas.

CHAPTER 1

RELATIONSHIPS AMONG LIVING THINGS

Can there ever be too much of a good thing? Unfortunately, the answer is *yes*. Take the fertilizer that helps crops grow. As useful as it is, fertilizer can also cause harm by running off into our water supply and damaging it. Relationships, or how one thing affects another, can be tricky!

PEOPLE USING SCIENCE

National Park Ranger In 1916 the National Park Service was created to preserve national parks. This agency relies on its team of park rangers to protect the wildlife and natural scenery within the parks.

Park rangers do many different jobs. Some rangers patrol the parks to make sure that visitors don't harm or otherwise change the environment. Other park rangers, such as Erin K. Broadbent, work to inform visitors of the history and importance of preserving the parks. As a park ranger in Washington, D.C., Erin Broadbent helps preserve the environments around the national monuments, such as the Washington Monument.

As you read Chapter 1, think about how changes in the environment affect the living things around you.

Coming Up

◀ Erin Broadbent realized her dream of working for the National Park Service.

WHAT DO LIVING THINGS NEED?

Imagine that it's a hot day and you're very thirsty. You need to drink a tall glass of water. Water is one of the things you need to live. Other living things need water, too. What else do living things need? In Investigation 1 you'll find out!

Activity

Needs of Plants

Plants seem to grow almost anywhere. What do they need to live?

Procedure

1. With a marker, write *Soil* on a paper cup containing a young plant growing in soil. Label a second such cup *Soil + Water*. Write *Soil + Water + Sunlight* on a third cup. Make a chart like the one shown.

Conditions	Plants After One Week
Soil	
Soil + Water	
Soil + Water + Sunlight	

2. Pour 25 mL of water into the cup labeled *Soil + Water*. Pour another 25 mL of water into the cup labeled *Soil + Water + Sunlight*.

See **SCIENCE** and **MATH TOOLBOX**
page H7 if you need to review
Measuring Volume.

3. Place the cup labeled *Soil* and the cup labeled *Soil + Water* in a place where the plants will get no light. Place the cup labeled *Soil + Water + Sunlight* near a window. **Predict** which conditions will be best for growth. **Record** your prediction in your *Science Notebook.*

4. Every day for one week, check that the soil is moist in the cup labeled *Soil + Water* and in the cup labeled *Soil + Water + Sunlight.* Do not add water to the cup labeled *Soil.*

5. After one week, **observe** the cups to see what the plants look like. **Record** your observations.

Step 4

Analyze and Conclude

1. Under which conditions did the young plants grow best? What did those plants have that the others did not?

2. How does your prediction compare with your results? From the class results, what can you **conclude** about some of the things plants need to live and grow?

INVESTIGATE FURTHER!

EXPERIMENT

What other questions can you ask about what helps plants to grow? Form a hypothesis and then plan an experiment to test it. After your teacher approves your plan, do the experiment. Share your results with your classmates.

Activity

A Pill Bug's Home

A pill bug's home keeps the pill bug safe and has the things it needs to live. Find out about two conditions that pill bugs need in this activity.

Procedure

1. Cover the bottom of a baking pan with paper towels. Tape the edges of the paper towels to the pan. Also seal with tape any places where the paper towels overlap. Place a sheet of newspaper over half of the top of the pan, as shown.

2. Use a spoon to carefully take 3 to 6 pill bugs, one by one, from their container and place them in the middle of the pan.

3. **Predict** whether the pill bugs will move toward light or away from light. **Record** your prediction in your *Science Notebook*. Shine a flashlight on the half of the pan not covered by newspaper. **Observe** where the pill bugs move. **Record** your observations.

Pill bug ▼

Step 1

E8

Step 4

4. Remove the sheet of newspaper. **Predict** whether pill bugs will move toward a dry area or a wet area. **Record** your prediction. Sprinkle water on the paper towels in half of the pan to make them moist. Leave the other half of the pan dry.

5. **Observe** where the pill bugs move. **Record** your observations. Carefully use a spoon to put the pill bugs back into their container.

Analyze and Conclude

1. How did your predictions compare with your results? Which do pill bugs prefer—light or darkness? Do they prefer moist, or dry, places?

2. From your results, what two conditions can you **infer** that pill bugs need in their homes?

3. Pill bugs live in the woods. If you went to the woods to look for them, **predict** where you would most likely find them.

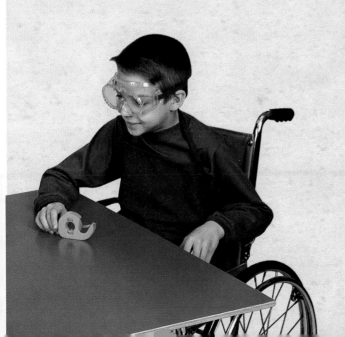

Technology Link
CD-ROM

INVESTIGATE FURTHER!

Use the **Best of the Net— Science CD-ROM**, Life Sciences, *The Bear Den and the Cub Den* to find out how bears adapt to their environment. You'll find out where bears live. And you'll learn what some bears do when the weather gets cold.

A Perfect Place to Live

Reading Focus How are the needs of living things alike, and how do their needs differ?

What do you really need? Perhaps you need a haircut. But you have more basic needs than that. Food, water, and air are some of the things you *really* need. Other living things need food, water, and air, too.

Living things also need a place to live. The place where an animal or a plant lives is its **habitat** (hab'i tat). Everything that surrounds and affects a living thing is its **environment** (en vī′rən mənt). All living things need an environment that is suited to their needs.

Salty or Not, Cold or Hot

Living things often have very different needs. So an environment that is good for one living thing may not be good for another. For example, all water animals need a water environment. But most dolphins need to live in salt water. The ocean is a good environment for most dolphins. Other water animals, such as lake trout, small-mouth bass, and minnows, would die in salt water. They need to live in the fresh water of lakes and streams.

This dolphin lives in the ocean. ▼

▲ Life in a freshwater lake

A spotted moray eel ▼

Some water animals need to live near the surface of the water, where light from the Sun keeps the water warm. Others need to live near the bottom. If you've ever gone fishing, you may know that bass need the warm water near the surface. But lake trout need the colder waters that are found at the bottom of a lake.

Many animals share the same habitat. The spotted moray eel lives in the warm, shallow ocean waters around coral reefs. Reef sharks, butterflyfish, batfish, and hogfish live in this habitat, too.

E11

Turn Off the Lights, Please!

Some living things need a lot of sunlight, and some need darkness. The activity on pages E6 and E7 proves that plants need sunlight to live. Without sunlight, plants couldn't make food and would die.

Different kinds of living things need different amounts of sunlight. For example, some kinds of flowers need shade. Other kinds need a lot of bright sunlight.

Pill bugs, which are observed in the activity on pages E8 and E9, need to live in a place that is dark and moist. Pill bugs will dry out in bright sunlight.

▲ A tropical rain forest in Costa Rica

Moles live underground. ▼

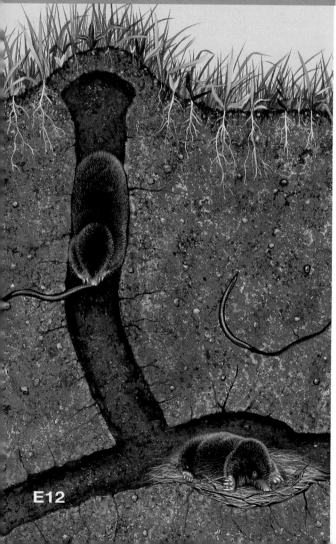

Some types of animals dig down into the soil to live in underground habitats. Animals such as earthworms need a dark, moist habitat. These animals would dry up and die in the bright, hot sunlight.

Moles also live underground. A mole is almost blind but has a keen sense of smell. A mole digs until it can smell the tiny insects and worms that are its food.

Very Wet or Very Dry

Some plants need a lot of rain, and others need almost no rain. The plants of the tropical rain forest need to be warm and wet. And they are! It rains almost every day of the year in the rain forest.

▲ Desert plants need very little rain.

Too Tiny to See

All living things need a suitable environment—even living things too small to see with just the eyes. Bacteria (bak tir′ē ə) are living things that can't be seen without a microscope. Bacteria are everywhere. They can be found living in soil, air, water, and even in your body. To survive, bacteria need a warm and wet environment.

From bacteria to whales, living things need an environment that meets their needs. You know that living things need food, water, and air. They also need a way to get rid of wastes. What needs do you have? ■

Other plants need a dry place to live. The teddy bear cholla, shown above, is a cactus that grows in the desert. It rains very little in the desert. But that's fine for a cactus. They don't need a lot of water.

Bacteria need warmth and moisture. ▼

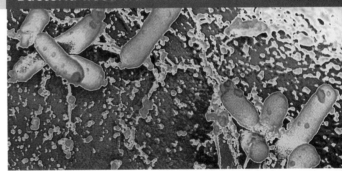

INVESTIGATION 1 WRAP-UP

REVIEW

1. Name three basic needs of living things.

2. How does a plant's or animal's environment help it to survive?

CRITICAL THINKING

3. Think about two different animals that have the same needs and live in the same habitat. What things in their environment would they compete for?

4. You plant grass in soil that is shaded by trees. The grass sprouts but turns yellow. What might be causing the problem?

INVESTIGATION 2

HOW DO LIVING THINGS GET THE FOOD THEY NEED?

When you are very hungry, what are your favorite foods? Living things get food in different ways. Where does your food come from? What are some ways other living things get food? Find out in Investigation 2!

Activity

MATERIALS

• *Science Notebook*

Meat and Potatoes

Do you eat plants, animals, or both? Find out by doing this activity.

What I Eat	
Food	From Plant or Animal

Procedure

In your *Science Notebook*, **make a chart** like the one shown. **Predict** whether most foods you eat come from plants or animals. For one week, **record** the kinds of foods you eat. List each part of a food and tell where it comes from. At the end of the week, share your observations with your classmates.

Analyze and Conclude

Do most of the foods you eat come from plants or from animals? How does your prediction compare with your findings?

Activity

A Menu for Molds

Do this activity to find out how living things called molds get food.

Procedure

1. Place one slice of moist bread and one slice of cheese in a sandwich bag. Seal the bag and tape it closed. Put the bag in a warm, dark place for one week. **Predict** what will happen to the foods in the bag. **Record** your prediction in your *Science Notebook*.

2. After one week, use a hand lens to **observe** the foods in the bag. Look for mold. *Do not open the bag.*

See **SCIENCE** and **MATH TOOLBOX** page H2 if you need to review *Using a Hand Lens.*

3. **Make drawings** of what you see. **Describe** how the food has changed.

4. Put the bag back in the same warm, dark place for another week. Repeat steps 2 and 3 at the end of the second week.

Analyze and Conclude

1. What happened to the food in the bag? **Compare** your prediction with your results.

2. From your results, **infer** what the molds you saw used for food.

3. **Predict** what would happen to the food if you left it in the bag for several months.

Step 1

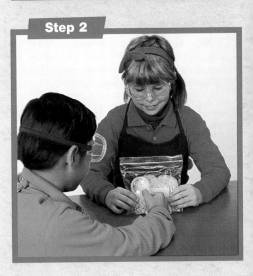

Step 2

What's for Dinner?

Reading Focus How can you classify living things by what they eat?

Plants make their own food. ▼

Imagine never needing to eat breakfast, lunch, or dinner! If you were a plant, you would never need to eat. You would make your own food.

Food Makers
Plants make their own food inside their leaves. Plants take in water and air from their environment. The leaves soak up sunlight. Plants use the Sun's energy to make food from water and a gas in the air. This food can be stored in roots, leaves, and other plant parts for use later on.

Living things that can make their own food are called **producers** (prō dōōs′ərz). Plants are producers. Producers make up the basic food supply in the environment. Without them, most other kinds of living things would not be able to exist.

May I See a Menu?
Since your body can't produce its own food, as a plant does, you have to get it another way—by eating something else. That means that you are a consumer (kən sōōm′ər).

A **consumer** is a living thing that eats plants, animals, or other living things.

What kinds of things are usually on your dinner plate? Crunchy crickets and other insects? You might eat these animals if you were a praying mantis. A praying mantis is an animal eater. Animals that eat only other animals are called **carnivores** (kär′nə vôrz). Spiders, many insects, and some worms are carnivores. Cats, snakes, wolves, owls, and many fish are carnivores, too.

◀ A praying mantis is a carnivore.

Wolves are carnivores. ▼

Brown bears sometimes eat plants. ▼

Prairie dogs do not eat other animals. They crawl out of their underground burrows and feed on plants. Marine iguanas (i gwä′nəz) also eat only plants, enjoying a meal of salty seaweed. Animals such as prairie dogs and marine iguanas are called herbivores (hʉr′bə vôrz). A **herbivore** is an animal that eats only plants. Elephants and horses are herbivores. So are caterpillars and deer. What other plant-eating animals can you think of?

Many animals are omnivores (äm′ni vôrz). **Omnivores** are animals that eat both plants and animals. Brown bears are omnivores. They eat berries and other fruits, but they also eat small animals, like fish.

Raccoons are also omnivores. So are some types of mice, birds, and turtles. The activity on page E14 investigates whether the food people eat comes from plants, animals, or both. If you eat both plants and animals, you're an omnivore, too!

Breaking It Down

In every environment there is an important group of consumers called decomposers (dē kəm pōz′ərz). **Decomposers** feed on the remains of once-living things. Bacteria, mushrooms, yeast, and molds are decomposers. Molds grow on foods that haven't been stored in the right way. Mold is grown in the activity on page E15. What can you do to prevent molds from growing?

Brown bears eat fish, too. ▼

▲ A raccoon is an omnivore.

Decomposers are important to the environment. They break down materials from once-living things into simpler materials. Decomposers release these simpler materials back into the water, soil, and air, where they can be used again by other living things. Rotting logs and rotting leaves on the forest floor are signs that decomposers have been at work. ■

Mushrooms are decomposers. ▶

Saber Teeth!

Reading Focus How were saber-toothed cats similar to African lions?

The cat watches its prey, waiting for the right moment to attack. Finally, it uses its short but powerful legs to leap onto the grazing animal. The heavy weight of the cat brings down its prey, a bison, in an instant. The cat uses its knifelike 23-cm (9-inch) teeth to slash into the belly of the bison.

This is no ordinary cat. It's a saber-toothed cat. But you won't see any of these cats around today. They became extinct around 11,000 years ago.

This bison, trapped in a tar pit, is about to be attacked by a saber-toothed cat. ▼

Extinction (ek stiŋk'shen) is the dying out of all living things of a certain kind. Can you think of any other animals that are extinct?

Scientists learn about saber-toothed cats by studying their remains, which are mostly preserved bones. Such remains are called fossils. Scientists have found many fossils in a place in California called the La Brea Tar Pits.

The La Brea Tar Pits is a bog, a place where the ground is wet and spongy. Water covers the bog. The tar pits contain a tarlike substance. Scientists have found thousands of bones from extinct animals, including saber-toothed cats, in the tar pits. Why are there so many fossils at La Brea?

▲ Compare the skull of the extinct saber-toothed cat to that of the modern African lion. What are the differences? What are the similarities?

Although saber-toothed cats are extinct, there are big cats alive today. These cats are something like those extinct cats. Compare the modern African lion, top right, to the saber-toothed cat, top left. They are both about the same size but the saber-toothed cat had shorter, more powerful legs. It also had a shorter tail and weighed almost twice as much as an African lion.

Scientists think that the saber-toothed cat hunted differently than a lion. It's likely that the saber-toothed cat was not as fast as today's big cats. It probably did not chase its prey. A saber-toothed cat most likely waited and watched for its prey to come close. When that prey came close enough, the big cat would pounce on it. ■

Internet Field Trip

Visit **www.eduplace.com** to learn more about how saber-toothed cats lived.

INVESTIGATION 2 WRAP-UP

REVIEW **1.** What is a producer? What is a consumer? Which one are you? Explain your answer.

2. Compare the diets of carnivores, herbivores, and omnivores.

CRITICAL THINKING **3.** Could carnivores live if all plants became extinct? Why or why not?

4. If scientists found the skeleton of an unknown animal, what clues would help them find out what kinds of foods the animal ate?

WHAT ARE FOOD CHAINS AND FOOD WEBS?

Slurp! The fast tongue of a frog catches a juicy fly. Gulp! A snake eats the frog. Will the snake become a meal for some other animal? In Investigation 3 you'll explore different eating relationships.

Activity

Making a Food-Chain Mobile

Do you eat hamburgers, fruit, and salad? No matter what you eat, you're part of a food chain. Do this activity to find out more about food chains.

MATERIALS

- books about plants and animals
- old magazines
- scissors
- crayons or colored markers
- tape
- yarn or string
- wire coat hanger
- *Science Notebook*

Procedure

1. In your *Science Notebook*, **make a list** of four living things. First, list one kind of plant. Then, think about the kind of animal that would eat that plant. List that animal. Next, think about an animal that would eat the animal you listed. List the second animal. Now do the same for a third animal. Get ideas by looking through animal books and magazines or from your own observations.

2. Cut out pictures from old magazines or **draw** pictures of the four living things in your food chain. Then tape your pictures to a piece of yarn, as shown. Put the living things in order of who eats whom. Think back to Investigation 2 to help you decide what should be at the bottom of your food chain. Tape the end of the yarn to a wire hanger. You've made a food-chain mobile.

Analyze and Conclude

1. Which living thing is the producer in your food chain?

2. Which living things are consumers?

3. Look at the food-chain mobiles of your classmates. What can you **infer** about the kind of living thing that is at the bottom of a food chain?

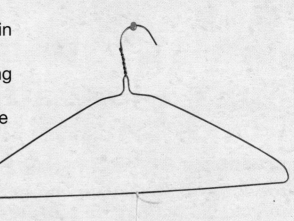

Step 2

Activity

More Links in the Food Chain

MATERIALS
- index cards
- crayons or colored markers
- short lengths of blue yarn and red yarn
- scissors
- *Science Notebook*

Most living things eat more than one kind of food. Because they do, many food chains may be linked together. In this activity you will play a game to see how food chains can link to form food webs.

- -

Procedure

1. Work in a group to write the names of the following living things on index cards, one per card: berries, nuts, water plants, mouse, snake, big fish, small fish, crayfish, owl, bear, chipmunk.

2. Place all the cards face up. With your group, arrange some of the cards to form a food chain.

3. Place a piece of blue yarn, about 10 cm long, on top of two cards so that each end is on a card. Use additional lengths of blue yarn to connect the other cards in the food chain.

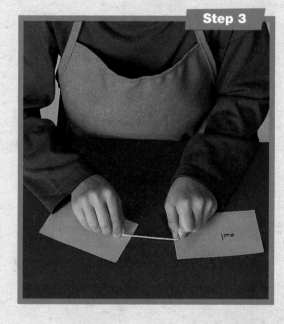
Step 3

Math Hint — *"About 10 cm" is an estimate. The length of yarn does not have to be exactly 10 cm.*

4. Use the remaining cards and blue yarn to create two more food chains.

5. Now look at the food chains you have made. Find a living thing in one food chain that can eat or be eaten by something in another food chain. Use a length of red yarn to connect these two cards.

E24

6. You have just linked two food chains together to form a food web. Find all the links between the food chains that you can. Connect the cards with lengths of red yarn. **Make a drawing** of your food web in your *Science Notebook*.

7. Look at the food webs made by other groups in your class. **Compare** these webs to the one your group made.

8. Think about what would happen if there were no producers. Take away the producer cards. **Infer** what would happen to the living things that eat the producers. **Infer** what would happen to the other members of the food web.

Analyze and Conclude

1. **Explain** how a food chain is different from a food web.

2. Suppose that most of the plants in a certain place die off. **Hypothesize** about what will happen to the animals that eat those plants.

UNIT PROJECT LINK

For this Unit Project you will make a mural of a tropical rain forest. Explore the producers of the different layers of the rain forest—the canopy, the understory, and the forest floor. With your classmates, make a mural showing different rain forest plants.

Technology Link

For more help with your Unit Project, go to **www.eduplace.com**.

Who Eats Whom?

Reading Focus What is the difference between a food chain and a food web?

A FOOD CHAIN

Plant

Grasshopper

Lizard

A grasshopper clings to a plant in the bright sunlight and nibbles on a leaf. Suddenly a lizard darts up from behind. It shoots out its tongue and eats the grasshopper. As the lizard slips away through the grass, a snake strikes and swallows the lizard whole. Later, an owl catches the snake and flies off to feed it to her young.

Food Chains

Every living thing needs food because food provides energy. When one animal eats another animal or a plant, they both become part of a food chain. A **food chain** is the path that energy takes as one living thing eats another. In the example above, the plant, grasshopper, lizard, snake, and owl are all connected to one another in a food chain. Cards are connected by yarn to show a food chain in the activity on pages E22 and E23. The plant, grasshopper, lizard, snake, and owl are all part of the same food chain.

Different environments, such as forests, deserts, or lakes, have different food chains. Some food chains are short, and some are long. But all food chains begin with a producer.

Links in the Chain

A plant is a producer and can make its own food. A producer is the first link in all food chains.

A consumer is the next link in a food chain. Animals are consumers. Some animals, such as grasshoppers, feed on plants. Then other animals, such as lizards, eat the animals that ate the plants.

Animals that hunt other animals for food are called **predators** (pred'ə tərz). The animals that are hunted by predators are called **prey**.

An animal can be both predator and prey. For example, a housefly may be eaten by a frog. In this case the frog is a predator. The fly is its prey. But the frog can become prey if a raccoon makes a meal of the frog.

▲ **A frog can be predator and prey.**

Likewise, the raccoon becomes prey if it's eaten by a predator, such as a cougar.

If no larger animal eats the cougar, does that mean the cougar is the top consumer in the chain? Not really. When the cougar dies, its body will become food for the last of the consumers—the decomposers. Bacteria, molds, and other decomposers feed on the remains of animals and break down these remains.

Snake

Owl

E27

A FOOD WEB

Grass is eaten by a rabbit.

A rabbit is eaten by a hawk.

A rabbit is eaten by a snake.

A snake is eaten by a hawk.

▲ What animals compete for the same food?

Chains Tangle Into Webs

There are some simple food chains in nature. But usually two or more food chains overlap and link, forming a **food web**. A model of a food web is made in the activity on pages E24 and E25.

A forest food web might include an oak tree. When the oak tree drops its acorns, hungry squirrels may eat the acorns and collect some for winter. Deer, mice, shrews, bears, and raccoons also eat acorns.

But acorns are not the only food these animals eat. Deer also eat grass, leaves, moss, twigs and other plant parts. Mice also nibble on grass and eat insects and spiders.

Grass is eaten by a grasshopper.

A grasshopper is eaten by a frog.

A frog is eaten by a bass.

A bass is eaten by a heron.

Small fish are eaten by a bass.

Raccoons also eat frogs, fish, fruit, crabs, grasshoppers, and sometimes even bird eggs.

You can see that in a large food web, many animals are connected to one another by the kinds of foods that they eat. Food webs show that every kind of living thing depends on other kinds of living things. Wherever you look in nature—in forests, lakes, meadows, oceans, or deserts—plants and animals are connected to one another through a web of life. ■

Internet Field Trip

Visit **www.eduplace.com** to learn about the food webs that spiders depend on for survival.

Cane Toads in Leaping Numbers

Reading Focus How did cane toads change the food chains and food webs in Australia?

Did you ever make a problem worse by trying to fix it? That's what happened in Australia in 1935. At that time, scientists thought they had discovered a way to get rid of the insects that were eating their crops. The result of their action was a country covered with huge toads, called cane toads. Cane toads may be as much as 23 cm (9 in.) long!

Cane toads live in Hawaii and other parts of the tropics. In 1935, scientists brought a group of cane toads to Australia to eat the beetles that were destroying the sugar cane crops. The scientists' idea might have worked except for one problem. The beetles' habitat is inside the sugar cane plants, but the toads' habitat is on the ground. Their paths never crossed, so the toads never ate the beetles.

Using Math *This cane toad shown is life-size. How does the size of this cane toad compare with the size of your hand?*

Although the cane toads didn't solve the beetle problem, they did make a difference. The toads changed the natural community (kə myoo'nə tē). A **community** is a group of plants and animals that live in the same area and depend on one another. When an animal is added to or taken away from a community, the food chains and food webs change.

The cane toads became part of the food chains and food webs in their new home. The huge toads gobbled up many of Australia's native lizards, snakes, mice, and birds. Scientists became worried about the possible extinction of these native animals.

The toad problem quickly became worse. Cane toads were laying up to 20,000 eggs at a time. And the toads had no natural predators. That's because the toads can protect themselves from being eaten by releasing poison from their necks. The native animals that tried to eat them were often poisoned to death!

In spite of the trouble they've caused, cane toads have become part of the culture in Australia. Some people consider them a tourist attraction. One politician even suggested putting up a statue to honor the cane toad! What do you think? Is Australia's cane toad a pet or a pest? ■

Science in Literature

GRASS EATERS RUN FOR LIFE!

One Small Square: African Savanna
by Donald M. Silver
Illustrated by
Patricia J. Wynne and Dianne Ettl
W. H. Freeman & Co., 1994

"The African savanna is home to the biggest, the tallest, and the fastest land animals on earth. It is where killer dogs work together as a team, and tiny termites build nests as high as the ceiling in your room and as hard as cement. One minute all is calm. The next, there is panic as thousands of grass eaters run for their lives."

More interesting facts can be found in the book *One Small Square: African Savanna* by Donald M. Silver. Enjoy fun activities while you explore life in the dangerous savanna.

Deadly Links

Reading Focus What caused the brown pelican to become endangered?

Suppose insects were destroying tomato plants you were growing. What would you do? You might spray an insecticide (in sek'tə sīd) on the plants to kill the insects. Insecticides are chemicals used to destroy insects that harm plants or carry diseases.

Killing Pests

Insecticides have been used widely throughout the world. Insecticides can help farmers keep crops growing healthy and strong. But these chemicals may remain in the soil for years. Some insecticides sprayed before you were born may still be in the soil today!

▲ **Insecticides can help crops grow.**

Through research, scientists found out that insecticides can harm more than the pests they were made to kill. The poisonous chemicals can be carried off by wind and moving water to new places. Once in these new places, the chemicals can harm wildlife. This was the case with DDT, an insecticide. DDT can kill many kinds of flies and mosquitoes that carry diseases. Even though DDT was useful for killing pests, it had harmful effects on other animals, such as the bald eagle and the brown pelican.

The STS logo image:

Follow the path of chemicals through this food chain. The addition of chemicals can cause changes in food chains, too. ▼

Pelican Problems

In California, DDT came close to killing all of the state's brown pelicans during the 1960s and 1970s. Scientists found that DDT from a factory was carried off in the waste water from the plant. Some of this waste water ended up in ocean waters. There the DDT was taken in by fish. When the brown pelicans ate these fish, the birds took DDT into their own bodies.

As DDT moves along a food chain, it is stored in the bodies of animals for a long time. When the brown pelicans laid their eggs, the DDT stored in the parent birds' bodies caused most eggs to have very thin shells. Most shells broke before the baby pelicans could grow. Because of DDT, there were hardly any new baby brown pelicans during those years. So the number of brown pelicans greatly decreased.

Brown pelicans on the East Coast and in Louisiana were also being harmed by DDT. In Louisiana the brown pelican had been named the state bird back when there were close to 100,000 pelicans in the state. Because of DDT, pelicans in Louisiana disappeared completely!

▲ DDT caused brown pelicans to lay eggs with very thin shells.

The Start of a Solution

In 1970 the pelican was listed as endangered. Something had to be done, or there would be no brown pelicans left. Finally, DDT was banned in the United States in 1972. Since then the number of pelicans has been on the rise.

Pelicans were not the only birds that were harmed by DDT. Bald eagles and peregrine falcons also laid eggs with thin shells because of the DDT stored in their bodies.

The law preventing the use of DDT has helped each of these great birds recover from the harmful chemical. But other countries still use DDT.

Although the use of DDT has been banned in the United States, there is still a need for insecticides. Today farmers use safer chemicals in smaller amounts. This means there is far less harm to the environment than with the use of DDT. ■

INVESTIGATION 3 WRAP-UP

REVIEW

1. What is the difference between a food chain and a food web?

2. Can an animal be a predator and also prey? Explain your answer.

CRITICAL THINKING

3. Think about the different things you eat and where they come from. Draw a diagram that shows you as part of a food web.

4. You see a sign that says, "Our new insecticide kills all bugs!" Do you think buying this product is a good idea or a bad idea? Explain your answer.

REFLECT & EVALUATE

Word Power

Write the letter of the term that best matches the definition. *Not all terms will be used.*

1. Path that energy takes as one thing eats another
2. Animal that eats plants and other animals
3. Living things that make their own food
4. Everything that surrounds and affects a living thing
5. Animal that hunts another animal for food
6. Place where an animal lives

a. carnivore
b. environment
c. food chain
d. food web
e. habitat
f. omnivore
g. predator
h. producers

Check What You Know

Write the term in each pair that best completes each sentence.

1. Bacteria, mushrooms, and molds are (producers, decomposers).
2. Two food chains that overlap form (a food web, an environment).
3. A living thing that eats plants, animals, or other living things is (a consumer, a predator).
4. Animals that are hunted are (predators, prey).

Problem Solving

1. Some animals are herbivores, others are carnivores, and still others are omnivores. Which are you? How do you know? Use the definitions of all three terms in your answer.

2. Suppose a tree near your home dies. Explain how this may cause changes in a food chain.

BUILD YOUR PORTFOLIO

Study the drawings. Explain how a frog can be both predator and prey.

CHAPTER 2

ADAPTATIONS OF LIVING THINGS

To survive, or stay alive, plants and animals need to have food. They need to protect themselves from danger, too. How could a good sense of hearing help an animal get food? What part of a plant could stop a hungry animal from eating it?

PEOPLE USING SCIENCE

Aquarium Curator Would you like to give a 200-pound harbor seal a dental exam? That's one of the jobs that Rhona St. Clair-Moore did while working at the Thomas H. Kean New Jersey State Aquarium where she headed the marine mammal program. She was also the first woman to be named curator (kyōō rāt'ər) at the aquarium. A curator is a person in charge of a section of a museum, library, or aquarium.

Rhona St. Clair-Moore says she has always liked animals. "When I was young, I watched nature shows with my father. I asked questions about animals." Her interest led her to follow a career at the aquarium.

In this chapter you'll read how many kinds of living things survive in their environment.

Coming Up

INVESTIGATION 1

HOW ARE LIVING THINGS ADAPTED FOR GETTING FOOD?
. . . . E38

INVESTIGATION 2

HOW ARE LIVING THINGS ADAPTED FOR PROTECTION?
. . . . E46

Rhona St. Clair-Moore blows a whistle when a seal is rewarded with food for good behavior. ▼

HOW ARE LIVING THINGS ADAPTED FOR GETTING FOOD?

A big eagle swoops down from the sky. It grabs a fish out of the water and flies away. How are eagles adapted to catch, carry, and eat fish? In Investigation 1 you'll explore many adaptations living things have for getting food.

Activity

The Right Beak for the Job

Why do birds have different kinds of beaks? How does a beak's shape help birds get food?

Procedure

1. Set up a pan with sand, as shown. Add water to the pan until it is two-thirds full.

2. Bury six to ten raisins in the sand. Sprinkle rice in the shallow water where the sand begins to slope upward.

3. Cut a plastic straw into five pieces. Place the pieces in the water so that they float.

Step 1

4. The raisins are models of small animals that live buried in the sand. The rice grains are small plants and animals that live in shallow water. The pieces of straw are models for fish. A toothpick, a plastic fork with taped tines, and a plastic soup spoon represent different kinds of bird beaks. In your *Science Notebook,* **predict** which beak is best for getting each kind of food.

5. **Make a chart** like the one shown. Use the toothpick to find and pick up raisins in the sand. **Count** the number of raisins you pick up in ten tries. **Record** this number in your chart. Now use the toothpick to pick up rice and then pieces of the straw. **Record** all your results in your chart.

Step 5

Kind of "Beak"	Number of Raisins	Number of Rice Grains	Number of Straw Pieces
toothpick			
fork			
spoon			

6. Replace the raisins, rice, and straw pieces. Repeat step 5, using the fork and then the spoon. **Describe** the methods you used with the different beaks and the different kinds of foods.

Analyze and Conclude

1. Which beak was best for collecting which food?

2. Think about the birds that would catch the plants and animals described in step 4. **Hypothesize** what each one's beak would look like. How is each bird's beak better than the models that you made?

3. **Infer** what birds with similar kinds of beaks have in common.

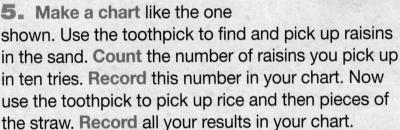

Technology Link CD-ROM

INVESTIGATE FURTHER!

Use the **Best of the Net—Science CD-ROM**, Life Sciences, *Miocene Sharks' Teeth of Calvert County* to learn more interesting facts about sharks. You'll find out about the many shark fossils dating back millions of years that geologists have found. And you'll learn how well sharks are adapted to their watery environment.

Catching Lunch

Reading Focus How do adaptations help living things get food?

When you say "I'm starved!" does someone make you a sandwich or snack? Animals in nature must find food in order to get a meal. Their task is made a little easier by the adaptations (ad əp tā'shənz) they have. **Adaptations** are behaviors or parts of living things that help the living things survive in a certain environment. Animals have adaptations for getting food. And so do some unusual plants.

It Makes Good Sense

Animals have special body parts that help them get food. Many animals have extraordinary vision, a super sense of hearing, or a sharp

This snake injects poison. ▼

sense of smell that helps them get food. Hunting birds, such as eagles and hawks, have very good eyes. They can spot prey from over a kilometer (half a mile) away! A dog's keen sense of smell can help uncover a tasty bone buried last year. The dog follows a scent trail that you couldn't smell at all! An owl, hunting at night, is able to swoop down on a mouse it can see running in the dark.

Deadly Weapons

Animals often have body parts that they can use as deadly weapons. A praying mantis clamps its front legs around butterflies, grasshoppers, and other insects before it eats them. Many snakes have fangs that can inject poison that can paralyze and kill their victims. A chameleon (kə mēl'ē ən) has a sticky lump on the end of its tongue that insects get trapped on. A brown bear uses sharp claws and teeth to catch and eat large fish.

E40

A Handy Tool!

The activity about bird beaks on pages E38 and E39 shows that some beaks are better for catching certain kinds of foods than other beaks. Woodpeckers use their pointed beaks to drill into trees so that they can catch insects.

An owl catches a deer mouse. ▼

Hummingbirds have long beaks and tongues that they use for sipping nectar from flowers.

Using Math

You can make your own nectar for hummingbirds by mixing 1 part sugar to 4 parts water. How many cups of sugar would you use with 8 cups of water?

The flamingo uses its bill as a strainer to trap tiny plants, shrimp, and snails found in shallow muddy waters. In the tropical rain forest, parrots and cockatoos use their strong beaks to crack nuts and seeds or to tear open fruit.

Mealtime Manners

You've seen how some body parts are adaptations for getting food. The behavior of an animal can also be an adaptation for getting food. **Behavior** is the way an animal typically acts in certain situations.

Electric eels, a kind of fish, have a really shocking way of getting food. They catch fish by stunning them with an electric shock! An archerfish catches an insect on a nearby water plant by using its long, tubelike mouthparts to shoot out water drops

An archerfish shoots water at an insect. ▼

that knock the insect into the water. Grasshoppers are able to hop more than a meter (about 3 ft) to search for a meal. That's 20 times the length of a grasshopper's body. If you had the muscle power of a grasshopper, you could jump about 24 m (80 ft)!

Some animals use tools from the environment to gather or eat food. While swimming on its back, the sea otter holds a rock on its belly and uses the rock to break open shells. Chimpanzees eat termites from a stick much the way you eat with a fork.

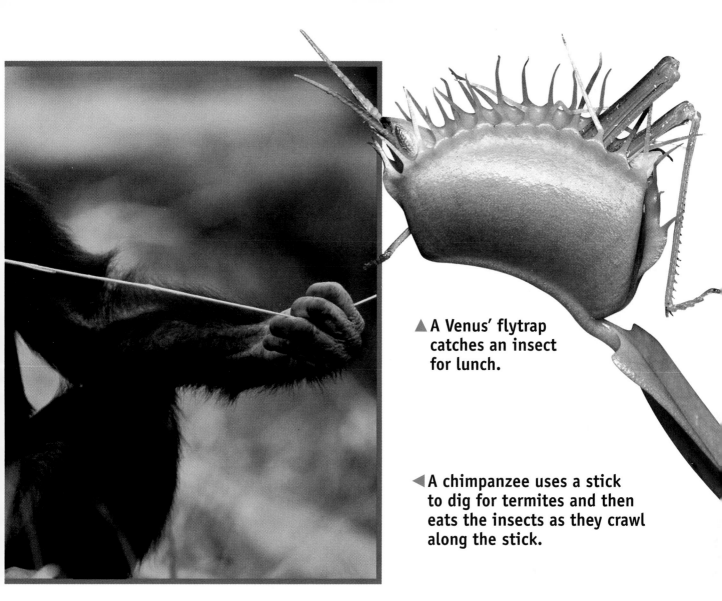

▲ A Venus' flytrap catches an insect for lunch.

◄ A chimpanzee uses a stick to dig for termites and then eats the insects as they crawl along the stick.

They peel the bark from a stick and poke it into a termite mound. When they pull out the stick, it is covered with tasty termite treats!

Other animals stalk, or secretly follow, their food. Have you ever watched a neighborhood cat sneak up on a bird? This method is the same one a leopard uses when it stalks a young gazelle on the African plain.

Plants That Trap Insects

Plants need certain nutrients (nōō′trē ənts). **Nutrients** are substances that provide materials needed for growth. Most plants absorb these nutrients from soil.

Plants have different adaptations to get these nutrients. The Venus' flytrap, sundew, and pitcher plants are known for "eating" insects. By trapping and digesting insects, these plants get nutrients that are missing from the soil in which they grow.

All living things need nutrients that food provides. You can see that plants and animals have many adaptations that help them get food. ■

A Quick Tongue

Reading Focus How is a chameleon adapted to its environment?

HOW IT Works

In the trees of a tropical forest, a chameleon walks along the branches in search of prey. The chameleon seems to be moving in slow motion. How can such a slow animal ever catch a fast-moving insect? The chameleon has some unusual adaptations for getting its food. Find out about them on these pages.

ODD EYES The chameleon's eyes look odd because each eye can move separately. With this adaptation, the chameleon can keep one eye on its prey while the other eye looks for predators.

WHAT A TAIL! A chameleon moves high up in the trees. If it loses its balance, it can curl its strong tail around a branch to keep from falling.

NEAT FEET The chameleon's foot has three toes joined on one side and two toes joined on the other side. The V-shaped foot is good for grabbing onto branches.

A TALENTED TONGUE The chameleon's tongue is very long—sometimes as long as its entire body. At the end of its tongue is a sticky patch that prey can get stuck on. When inside the chameleon's mouth, the tongue is folded much like an accordion. When prey comes within range, the chameleon shoots out its tongue. Its tongue moves so fast that it would be hard for you to see it move.

Difficult to Spot

The chameleon has a good chance of surprising its prey. That's because of **camouflage** (kam'ə-fläzh)—the ability to blend in with the surroundings. Besides helping the chameleon sneak up on its prey, camouflage makes it hard for predators to spot the chameleon. ■

INVESTIGATE FURTHER!

RESEARCH

Plants and animals have adaptations that help them survive. With a group, choose an animal from your community. What kinds of adaptations does it have? Create a poster of your animal describing its adaptations and show the poster to your classmates.

INVESTIGATION 1 WRAP-UP

REVIEW

1. Describe how body parts help living things get food.

2. Describe how behaviors help living things get food.

CRITICAL THINKING

3. Are humans the only living things that use tools? Argue for or against this theory based on the behaviors of sea otters and chimpanzees.

4. Invent an animal. Draw your animal, showing the kinds of adaptations it would have for getting food. Explain your animal's behavior for getting food.

How Are Living Things Adapted for Protection?

Danger! What do you do? Do you run or hide? Do you stand as still as you can? Living things have different adaptations to protect themselves. Find out about these adaptations in Investigation 2.

Activity

Blending In

Frogs, spiders, and birds are just a few of the predators that eat insects. How do insects protect themselves? This activity will help you find out.

MATERIALS
- colored paper
- colored markers, colored pencils, or crayons
- scissors
- tape
- *Science Notebook*

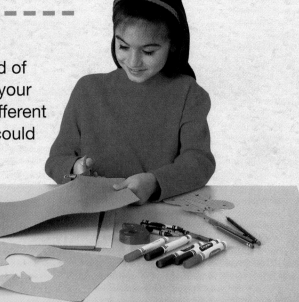

Procedure

1. Your job is to **design** and **draw** a new kind of insect—one that could hide from predators in your classroom. Look around your classroom for different colors, shapes, and patterns that your insect could blend with and not be easily seen.

2. To draw your insect, use any or all of the drawing materials listed. Remember, your insect must have camouflage so that it blends in and is hard to find.

Step 3

3. When you have finished drawing your insect, cut it out. Your teacher will tell you when to "hide" your insect. **Predict** where your insect will be hardest to find. Then put your insect in that place. If your insect hides on the wall, use a very small piece of tape to attach it. See if others can find it.

4. In your *Science Notebook,* **describe** what your insect looks like in its hiding place.

Analyze and Conclude

1. Which insect in your class was the hardest to find? **Hypothesize** why it was hard to find that insect.

2. **Infer** how the color, shape, or size of your insect helped it hide. **Explain** your answer.

3. **Predict** what would happen to an insect that didn't have any way to hide from predators. How might such an insect be able to survive?

UNIT PROJECT LINK

Research how animals of the tropical rain forest are adapted to their environment. Construct some rain forest animals and attach them to your mural. Make some camouflaged animals and "hide" them among the plants. Also attach predators and their prey to show a food web.

TechnologyLink
For more help with your Unit Project, go to **www.eduplace.com**.

Hiding Out and Other Defenses

Reading Focus What are some adaptations that help plants and animals protect themselves?

▲ Crab spider on flower

▲ Thornbugs on stem

▲ Tulip tree beauty moth on tree bark

You Can't See Me

Hide-and-seek is fun. But animals in nature must stay safe from enemies and catch food to eat. How they play the game can be a matter of life or death! The activity on pages E46 and E47 shows how camouflage is an important adaptation for defense for many animals. When a young spotted fawn is left alone, it can keep very still and blend in with the forest floor. This keeps predators from seeing the fawn.

An insect called a katydid has wings that look like the leaves of the trees it lives on. Its wings even have brown spots that look like spots found on real leaves. In the photos above, how does camouflage help the animals hide?

E48

The thorns on a rose are a sharp defense. ▼

Don't Come Too Close!

Some plants have sharp thorns or bristles that help protect them from being eaten. An animal that has nibbled on a sweet-smelling rose and gotten pricked by a thorn, for example, is not likely to make that mistake again.

Some plants contain poisonous or irritating chemicals that keep many animals away. Have you ever touched poison ivy or poison sumac? If so, you know that days of skin sores and itching can result. Because of these effects, many people have learned to stay away from these plants.

Sometimes a plant's defense is its bitter taste. For this reason, some people plant marigold plants around their vegetable gardens. Rabbits are often attracted to the bright orange and yellow colors of these flowers.

◀ **A katydid stays safe because predators mistake it for a leaf.**

A marigold's bitter taste keeps it safe from hungry animals. ▶

But after tasting the marigolds, the rabbits usually go elsewhere in search of more pleasant-tasting plants to nibble.

Animals that are covered with quills or spines have a defense against being eaten. No animal wants to eat quills or spines. The quills of porcupines and spines of hedgehogs provide prickly protection.

Most of the time a puffer fish does not look prickly. But when it is attacked, or when it fears attack, it can suck in water and blow itself up into a spine-covered ball. Its shape, size, and spines make it impossible for even a large fish to eat the puffer fish!

You're Copying Me!

Some animals are protected from enemies because they look like other, more dangerous, animals. Most wasps and hornets have black and yellow stripes. Animals that have been stung by these dangerous insects learn to avoid them. Some harmless beetles also have black and yellow stripes. These beetles may not be attacked by predators because they look like the more dangerous hornets and wasps.

Using Math *Do you think a porcupine is more likely to have 30 quills or 30,000 quills? Explain your answer.*

A relaxed puffer fish ▼   **An alarmed puffer fish under attack** ▼

Other copycats include the harmless kingsnake, which looks like the poisonous coral snake. Both snakes have red, yellow, and black stripes, but the colors are arranged differently. Although the creature on the right looks like a snake, it's actually a caterpillar from a Costa Rican rain forest. Some butterflies and moths fool predators because of two bright spots on their wings. The spots look like the eyes of large owls.

Tricked You, Didn't I?

The opossum is famous for tricking predators into thinking it's dead. The trick works because the opossum's enemies eat only freshly killed meat. The squid also tricks its enemy. It sprays an inklike substance in its enemy's face. This inky cloud prevents the enemy from seeing the squid. While the enemy is blinded, the squid swims away.

This caterpillar(*left*) and butterfly(*right*) scare away predators by looking like other animals.

The kingsnake (*right*) is a copycat of the poisonous coral snake (*left*).

E51

▲ **An ostrich protecting its young**

pounces on the tail and eats it while the rest of the lizard escapes!

Many birds pretend to be hurt to protect their chicks. The African ostrich flaps its wings and cries out when a predator heads toward its young. This gets the attention of the predator, which goes after the adult bird instead of the chicks.

Some lizards have a last-chance defense against predators by losing their tails! The tail continues to twitch after it has dropped off the lizard. This tricks the predator, which

Going My Way?

Some animal behaviors are adaptations for protection against parasites (par′ə sīts). **Parasites** are creatures that live on or in other living things and harm them. Adaptations that protect against parasites have led to some very unusual friendships.

Science in Literature

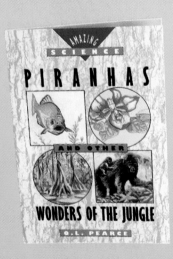

Piranhas and Other Wonders of the Jungle
by Q. L. Pearce
Illustrated by Mary Ann Fraser
Julian Messner, 1990

RIVER SHARK EATS COW!

"If you saw a list of the world's most dangerous fish, you would likely find the piranha near the top. . . . This fish is equipped with an arsenal of stabbing, cutting teeth. . . . An animal as large as a cow can be devoured in just a few minutes, leaving nothing but bare bones."

Discover more interesting facts about rain forest life in the book *Piranhas and Other Wonders of the Jungle* by Q. L. Pearce. Learn how different jungle creatures survive and protect themselves by adapting to their environment.

Birds called oxpeckers eat a meal off the hide of a rhinoceros. ▶

Oxpeckers, or tickbirds, are small African songbirds. These birds eat ticks and other annoying parasites off the tough skin of the rhinoceros, buffalo, and elephant. By allowing the birds to remain on them, these large animals protect themselves from parasites. In exchange, the birds are protected from predators as they dine. Few animals would attack a bird sitting on a fierce rhino.

Another unusual friendship occurs in coral reefs under the sea. A small fish called the cleaner fish removes parasites from the skin, gills, and mouth of many other reef fish. The coral reef fish are protected from parasites, and the cleaner fish has an easily found meal.

As you can see, plants and animals have many defenses. All are a matter of survival. ■

◀ **The arrows point to two cleaner fish eating parasites from a coral reef fish.**

Medicines From Nature

Reading Focus How is nature like a drugstore?

When you're sick, a family member probably gets you medicine from the drugstore. In some places, though, you might just be told, "Take a hike!"

Hitting the Nature Trail

People all over the world hike along woodland paths to find healing plants. They rely on nature's drugstore for relief. If you live in the Ozark Mountains of Missouri, your family might brew spicebush tea to bring down your fever. If you live in the Appalachian Mountains and have a stomachache, someone might serve you a gentle drink of slippery elm bark tea. This treatment was used by pioneers over 200 years ago.

Plants produce chemicals that help in their protection and survival. The chemicals are in leaves, bark, roots, blossoms, and seeds. The use of these chemicals as medicine goes back thousands of years.

Medicines From Living Things

Many plant parts and chemicals, as well as animal parts, have been used as medicines. The ancient Greeks used a powder made from substances in the bark of the willow tree to treat pain and reduce fever.

The main ingredient in aspirin is similar to a substance in the bark of the willow tree. ▶

ASPIRIN

In the 1890s a German chemist studied the substances in willow bark. In a laboratory, he developed a similar substance, aspirin. Today aspirin is probably the most-widely-used medicine in the world.

Early settlers in America often relied on medicines used by Native Americans. The Cherokees used the bark of the sassafras tree to treat sores. They then applied a soothing paste of powdered maize, or corn, and soft turkey down feathers!

Navajo (nav′ə hō) healers still use the root of the strong-smelling osha plant. Not only does osha root help treat colds, but it also has been found to keep snakes away.

▲ **The Ohlone people in California use the roots of the horsetail plant to make a syrup for coughs.**

A Cherokee helps heal an early settler with bark and powdered maize. ▶

In some places, people use snakes as part of a cure. Some shops in China offer medicines made from snake blood, venom, and skin to improve vision.

Natural First-Aid Kit

Some people keep an aloe plant in the kitchen. Burns from cooking can be soothed by breaking off a fleshy aloe leaf and squeezing its clear liquid onto the burns.

Today nearly half of all prescribed drugs contain at least one chemical from nature. Scientists have climbed mountains and crossed deserts in their search for plants that can be used to produce new medicines.

Scientists are hopeful that many discoveries will be made in tropical rain forests. Most plants in the rain forests haven't yet been identified. The search for medicines from nature continues. ■

Plants and animals of the rain forest may hold new cures. ▶

An aloe plant ▼

INVESTIGATION 2 WRAP-UP

REVIEW

1. Describe two protective adaptations found in plants.

2. How does camouflage protect an animal?

CRITICAL THINKING

3. Is an animal's ability to learn an adaptation? Explain your answer.

4. Imagine you are walking through a forest to observe the animals that live there. Describe some of the adaptations the animals might have to protect themselves.

REFLECT & EVALUATE

CHAPTER 2 REVIEW

Word Power

Write the letter of the term that best matches the definition. *Not all terms will be used.*

1. The way an animal acts
2. Creatures that live on or in other living things and harm them
3. Behaviors or parts of living things that help them survive
4. Ability to blend in with the surroundings

a. adaptations
b. behavior
c. camouflage
d. nutrients
e. parasites

Check What You Know

Write the term in each pair that best completes each sentence.

1. The shape of a bird's beak is an adaptation for (getting food, protection).
2. By digesting an insect, a Venus' flytrap gets (parasites, nutrients).
3. An opossum pretending to be dead is an example of an adaptive (behavior, body part).
4. An adaptation that helps protect a rose plant is its (leaves, thorns).
5. A cleaner fish eats (predators, parasites) from coral reef fish.

Problem Solving

1. A rabbit begins to eat a plant. But after one bite, the rabbit won't ever eat that plant again. Explain an adaptation the plant might have that protects it from being eaten by the rabbit.
2. Some animals hunt food only at night. The darkness may protect them from predators, but how do they find their food in the dark? Explain how certain senses might be adaptations that help these animals find food in the dark.

Study the photograph of the lobster. What adaptations does the lobster have for catching food or for protecting itself?

CHAPTER 3

LIVING THINGS IN THE ENVIRONMENT

What living things change the environment the most? If you guessed humans, you're right. And right now people are very quickly changing the country of Brazil. Some of those changes are destroying the environments of plants and animals.

PEOPLE USING SCIENCE

Wildlife Photographer Luiz Claudio Marigo is a Brazilian wildlife photographer. Many of the animals and plants in his photographs no longer exist. His pictures are all that are left of them.

But Luiz Marigo is doing more than recording vanishing animals and their forest homes. He is trying to show his country's wonderful wildlife. Luiz Marigo wants people to save Brazil's forests.

Luiz Marigo's interest in photography began as a child on his first trip to a wildlife area. He knew at once that he would devote himself to capturing nature with his camera.

As you read this chapter, think about the living things that share your environment. How do changes affect the plants, animals, and people around you?

▲ Luiz Claudio Marigo

Coming Up

◀ **A photo by Luiz Marigo of two Brazilian jaguars**

E59

How Can Living Things Change the Environment?

Have you ever seen a house being built? Big machines are used to move dirt and cut down trees. In Investigation 1, find out how people and other living things change their environments.

Activity

My Neighborhood Keeps Changing!

Think about an old photograph that shows your home or neighborhood. Then think about your home or neighborhood as it is today. What changes have taken place? How do people make changes to their environments?

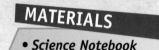

Dallas, Texas in 1908 ▼

Procedure

1. **Observe** the two pictures on page E61. The neighborhood shown has changed in many ways over the years. In your *Science Notebook*, **make a list** of all the changes you can find. **Compare** your list with those of other group members to see if there is anything that you missed.

Step 1

2. Look at your list. Infer who made the changes. Talk with your group and hypothesize how the changes affected living things in the area.

Analyze and Conclude

1. What caused the changes in this neighborhood? Explain how these changes affected the environment.

2. Think about the neighborhood that you live in. Predict what your neighborhood will look like when you grow up. How might people and other living things change your neighborhood?

INVESTIGATE FURTHER!

RESEARCH

Tape-record sounds from your neighborhood. Then bring the tape to school. Have your classmates identify which sounds are made by nature and which are made by people. Hypothesize what your neighborhood may have sounded like 100 years ago.

Busy Beaver Construction Co.

People build dams to control the flow of water from rivers and streams. The beavers of North America, without any training in construction, or building, do the same thing. These hard-working animals build dams and keep them in repair.

Timber!

Beavers do a lot of work to build a dam. They use their sharp teeth to chew away at the trunks of trees. Beavers can chomp through a tree trunk 1 m (3 ft) thick! The trees come crashing down. Then the beavers cut the trunks and branches into logs, again using their sharp teeth. They float the logs into position in the stream. Then they cement the logs together with mud, stones, and leaves.

A Warm, Dry Lodge

Beavers build dams across the moving waters of streams and rivers. The dams create ponds. In the still water of the ponds, beavers build their habitat—a lodge. A lodge is a small living area made of tree parts and mud. The lodge rises up from the pond. The lodge protects a group of beavers from cold weather and from predators.

A Home for Others

The ponds created by dams become homes for other animals, too. Many kinds of fish as well as insects, spiders, frogs, and salamanders live in the quiet ponds. Water birds build nests near the ponds. Many of these animals would not be able to make their homes in streams that lacked dams.

dam

A Changed Place

Beavers cut down many trees along the shore to build their dams and lodges. When the beavers have cut down most of the trees near the pond, they move. They leave behind the results of their hard work and start all over again.

Over time, the ponds created by beaver dams fill with rich soil. They become beautiful meadows. Plants such as grasses and wildflowers grow in the meadows. By cutting down trees, building dams, creating ponds, and making lodges, beavers greatly change the environment. ■

The beavers enter their lodge through an underwater tunnel. ▼

lodge

People Change the Environment

Reading Focus How can changes people make to the wetlands be helpful and harmful?

What would the world look like without the changes people have made? There would be no buildings, no streets, and no highways. What else would be different?

The activity on pages E60 and E61 shows old and new pictures of a neighborhood. The changes were caused by the activities of people.

Too Wet

A place where living and nonliving things interact is called an **ecosystem**. Sometimes people change an ecosystem because they want to use land for farming or to build on. But not all land is suitable for these purposes. For example, some land may be too wet.

Science in Literature

Piranhas and Other Wonders of the Jungle
by Q. L. Pearce
Illustrated by Mary Ann Fraser
Julian Messner, 1990

KILLER ANTS MARCH!

"One of the most frightful creatures in Central Africa is less than one inch long. Feared by humans and animals alike, it is the driver ant. In a single colony, there may be up to 20 million biting ants, and once they have begun their march, nothing in their path is safe."

Read about how these dreaded ants are used to help people in the book *Piranhas and Other Wonders of the Jungle* by Q. L. Pearce.

Building on wetlands is an example of a change that people have made to an ecosystem. **Wetlands** include swamps, marshes, and bogs. People drain the water from wetlands to use the land for farming, housing, and industry. Today, less than half the wetlands in the United States remain.

The wetlands are home to birds, insects, fish, snakes, beavers, and a large variety of plants. When people change wetland environments, many living things may lose their homes.

Making Things Better

People also make changes that improve their environments. Many people are working together to protect the world's wetlands. Some people even fill wetlands with water during long periods of dry weather.

People create new parks in which animals and plants are protected. They plant trees and gardens that become new homes for many different living things. In many ways, people are always changing the natural environment. ■

Giants Stadium in New Jersey (left) *was built on wetlands. The Everglades are wetlands in Florida* (right). *The original 48 states contained a total of 215 million acres of wetlands. Only 95 million acres remain. How many acres of wetlands have been lost?*

Bringing Back the Buffaloes

Reading Focus What caused buffaloes to nearly disappear, and why have their numbers increased?

Long ago the Great Plains of the United States and Canada were covered with large roaming herds of American bison, also called buffaloes. But the large herds of buffaloes began to disappear. And so did the prairies, or grasslands, they once roamed.

People changed much of the prairie land to make it suitable for building and farming.

But today, even without their old prairie land, the buffaloes are back in growing numbers. Take a trip back in time to find out why the buffaloes almost disappeared and how they've come back.

All buffaloes east of the Mississippi River have been killed.
1800

The horse arrives in North America, brought by Spanish explorers. By using horses, the people of the Great Plains learn how to ride and hunt, making it easier to kill buffaloes.
1600

1880
Hundreds of hunters wipe out the buffaloes of the Canadian plains.

Several thousand buffaloes are moved to Wood Buffalo National Park in Alberta, Canada.

1920

BEYOND 2000

1990s

Because they are protected, buffaloes are no longer in danger of becoming extinct.

Yellowstone National Park

1894

The buffalo is nearly extinct.
Theodore Roosevelt, who would later become President of the United States, wants to protect the buffalo. Congress passes a law against killing buffaloes. The herds slowly begin to grow again.

According to the National Bison Association, there are over 200,000 buffaloes in the United States. In Canada, the total number of buffaloes is expected to reach 120,000 by the year 2000.

Today, most buffaloes are in parks because the prairie land they once roamed has been changed. Farmland, factories, towns, and roads have replaced much of the old prairies. ■

_____ **INVESTIGATION 1 WRAP-UP** _____

THINK IT WRITE IT

REVIEW

1. Explain how an animal can change its environment. Explain how people change their environments.

2. Give three examples of wetlands.

CRITICAL THINKING

3. You observe that a large part of a tropical rain forest has been cut down. How might such a change affect the living things in that area? Explain your answer.

4. Give an example of two living things that have different habitats but live in the same ecosystem.

HOW ARE LIVING THINGS ADAPTED TO THEIR ENVIRONMENTS?

Why do you sweat when your environment is hot and shiver when it's cold? These are examples of adaptations. In Investigation 2, discover other ways living things are adapted to their environments.

Activity

Keeping Heat In

Adaptations help living things survive. In this activity find out how some animals are adapted to cold weather.

MATERIALS

- 2 large plastic jars
- 2 small plastic jars
- down feathers
- hot tap water
- 2 thermometers
- timer
- *Science Notebook*

SAFETY

Clean up spills immediately.

Procedure

1. In this activity, you'll make models of two animals. One has feathers. The other one does not. Talk with your group and predict which animal model will lose more heat in 30 minutes. Record your prediction in your *Science Notebook*.

2. Make a chart like the one shown.

Time (in min)	Temperature (°C) Model With Feathers	Temperature (°C) Model Without Feathers
0		
15		
30		

3. To make your models, place a small jar in a larger jar. Place down feathers around the small jar. Cover the sides of the small jar completely with feathers but don't pack the feathers tightly.

4. Place another small jar in a different larger jar. Don't put anything around this small jar.

5. Fill each small jar halfway with hot tap water. Take care not to wet the feathers. Put a thermometer in each small jar. **Measure the temperature** of the water in each jar. **Record** your readings under the correct heading on the first line in your chart.

Step 5

 See **SCIENCE** and **MATH TOOLBOX** page H8 if you need to review *Using a Thermometer.*

6. After 15 minutes, record the temperature of the water in each jar. Wait another 15 minutes. Then record both temperatures again.

Analyze and Conclude

1. By how many degrees did the temperature in each jar change?

2. Which animal model lost more heat? How does this result compare with your prediction?

3. Study your models. **Hypothesize** about how down feathers help a bird stay warm.

Technology Link CD-ROM

INVESTIGATE FURTHER!

Use the **Best of the Net—Science CD-ROM**, Life Sciences, *Bristlecone Pine* to find out about the discovery of ancient bristlecone pine trees, the oldest living things on Earth. Find out how growth rings reveal changes in Earth's environment.

Beating the Heat

Reading Focus How are different plants and animals adapted to desert environments?

Both animals and plants have adaptations that protect them from extreme heat. On a blazing hot day in summer, what do you do to stay cool? To protect your skin from burning in the sunlight and your body from overheating, you'd likely head for a shady spot.

Your body has a built-in way of cooling down. In hot weather your skin becomes covered with tiny droplets of perspiration, or sweat. The ability to sweat is an adaptation that helps prevent overheating. When sweat dries up, the drying process cools your skin.

Although sweating is an important adaptation to humans, few other animals sweat. In a desert, if an animal did sweat, it would quickly become dried out. There is little water available in the desert to replace the body's lost moisture.

Life in the Desert

How does a desert animal, which lives where the Sun scorches the sand all day, survive? There are no tall leafy trees for shade. In some deserts, daytime air temperatures can reach 55°C (131°F). Rain is scarce, and there are few water holes to drink from. Deserts may seem to be impossible places to live in. But, amazingly, the world's deserts are home to thousands of kinds of plants and animals. All have adaptations to "beat the heat."

Using Math *In the Namib Desert in Africa, shown here, surface temperatures can reach as high as 77°C (170°F). Compare this temperature to the daytime air temperature in the desert, given in the text above.*

Insects Keep Cool

Some desert insects have body designs that keep them cool. One little beetle that lives in the Namib Desert of southwestern Africa survives by keeping its body away from the hot sand. How does it do this? Nicknamed the stilt beetle, this insect "tiptoes" over sun-baked sand dunes on long stiltlike legs.

The black color of some beetles can be a problem in the desert. This is because dark-colored material heats faster than does light-colored material. Many desert beetles have white or yellow wax covering their dark bodies. The light-colored wax reflects sunlight, keeping the insect's body cool. Because wax is water-proof, the waxy covering also helps hold in moisture, keeping the beetle from drying out.

What characteristics of a stilt beetle help it survive in the desert?

Never Thirsty

The behaviors of desert animals are also adaptations to the hot, dry environment. Kangaroo rats have some unusual adaptations for conserving water. A kangaroo rat may go its entire life without ever taking a drink of water! Kangaroo rats get moisture from the food they eat— seeds, juicy grasses, and the pulp of cactus plants. These animals don't sweat, and they are active only at night.

Internet Field Trip

Visit **www.eduplace.com** to find out how desert animals have adapted to their dry environments.

▲ A kangaroo rat burrows in the sand to stay cool during the day.

The saguaro cactus grows in deserts of the southwestern U.S. and northern Mexico. ▼

During the day, kangaroo rats sleep sealed inside their "cool" burrows. Their burrows are about 0.3 m (1 ft) below the desert sand. Since the Sun doesn't heat this sand directly, the temperature in the burrow is a cool 30°C (86°F).

Hidden Water

Plants also have adaptations to the hot, dry desert environment. Cactus plants hold a lot of water inside. They have thick stems and slender, spiny leaves that keep in moisture. Cactus roots are widespread just beneath the desert's surface. These shallow roots can rapidly take in water from a rare desert rainfall before the sunlight causes the water to dry up. Then the water is stored for weeks inside the cactus.

The largest kind of cactus is the saguaro (sə gwär'ō). After years of growing slowly, a saguaro can reach 15 m (50 ft) in height and can store hundreds of liters of water. ■

A flowering saguaro cactus ▼

UNIT PROJECT LINK

Another environment that you have read about in this unit is the tropical rain forest. Tropical rain forests have many important resources. Find out why tropical rain forests are disappearing. Make a poster that lists things you and your friends can do to help save the rain forests.

Technology Link

For more help with your Unit Project, go to **www.eduplace.com**.

When the Going Gets Tough...

> **Reading Focus** What adaptations do some plants and animals have to survive cold winters?

Maple trees drop their leaves, robins fly south, and woodchucks curl up in dens and go into a deep sleep. These things all happen as the cold of winter approaches. Why?

In nature there are many cycles—summer and winter, rainy season and dry season, and others. These natural cycles happen in different places around the world. Sometimes a cycle creates big changes in the environment. Then plants and animals have to change in some way, too, in order to survive.

Winter Travel

How can an animal survive through a cold, snowy winter if it can't find enough food to eat? One way is for the animal to **migrate** (mī′grāt), or travel to a warmer place where it can find food.

Many kinds of birds migrate. It's not the cold weather that makes them leave. The activity on pages E68 and E69 shows that feathers help birds stay warm. Some birds can survive cold weather if they can find enough food.

The lesser golden plover and the Arctic tern are two kinds of birds that migrate. ▼

equator

▲ **Lesser golden plover**

Some seed-eating birds, such as blue jays and cardinals, don't migrate.

But insect-eating birds and birds whose food is often covered by snow or ice usually migrate before winter comes. Some fly long distances. The lesser golden plover migrates over 3,200 km (2,000 mi)—from Alaska to Hawaii. And the Arctic tern migrates about 20,000 km (12,000 mi)—from the Arctic in the north to the Antarctic in the south!

▲ A chipmunk hibernates through most of the winter but may wake up on warmer days to eat.

◄ Arctic tern

Winter Sleep

How *else* do animals survive a cold winter without food? Some animals go into a deep sleep, called **hibernation** (hī bər nā′shən). Bears, ground squirrels, woodchucks, snakes, and bats all may hibernate during winter.

While an animal is in this deep sleep, its body temperature usually drops. Its heartbeat rate slows, and it breathes less. All these changes mean that an animal uses up less energy. Therefore, it can survive a long time without eating.

When warmer weather returns, the animal begins to warm up, too. Its heart starts beating faster, and soon it wakes up—to spring and a new supply of food!

Plants in Winter

Plants are rooted to one spot, so they can't migrate. But their activities can slow, as if they were going into a deep sleep. This decrease in plant activity is called **dormancy** (dôr′mən sē). Plants become dormant during the winter.

As winter approaches, many trees—such as maples, oaks, poplars, elms, and chestnuts—lose their leaves. Without leaves, a tree can't make food. So, during dormancy the tree lives off food that is stored elsewhere in the plant—for example, in the roots.

Some plants, such as ferns, die above ground. But their roots survive underground through winter. When the weather warms up, the plants begin to grow again. ■

▲ Each autumn, trees like this maple lose their leaves.

INVESTIGATION 2 WRAP-UP

REVIEW

1. Describe one adaptation of an animal and one adaptation of a plant for survival in the desert.

2. Compare hibernation and dormancy.

CRITICAL THINKING

3. There is snow on the ground and on tree branches and bushes. You see only one or two kinds of birds. What adaptation do the birds have for keeping warm? Why did other kinds of birds leave?

4. What adaptation do you have to beat the heat? Do most desert animals have the same adaptation? Explain your answer.

REFLECT & EVALUATE

Word Power

Write the letter of the term that best completes each sentence.

a. dormancy
b. hibernation
c. migrate
d. wetlands

1. Environments that include swamps, marshes, and bogs are ——.
2. To travel to a warmer place to find food is to ——.
3. A decrease in activity in plants during winter is called ——.
4. Some animals go into a deep winter sleep called ——.

Check What You Know

Write the term in each pair that best completes each sentence.

1. When people change environments, many living things may lose their (adaptations, homes).
2. Sweating is an adaptation for keeping (wet, cool).
3. When food is scarce, some birds (migrate, hibernate).
4. While an animal hibernates, its heartbeat rate (slows down, speeds up).

Problem Solving

1. A family on vacation decides to go scuba diving. The group leader tells the family not to take any of the plants and animals from their underwater environment. Why is it important for the divers not to change the underwater environment?

2. Brown bears build up fat in their bodies before hibernating. How is this an adaptation?

Study the drawing. List all the ways that the beavers changed their environment. How did these changes affect other animals?

Compare and Contrast

When you read, ask if two or more things, events, or ideas are being compared. Look for signal words that tell how things are alike and how they are different.

Read the paragraphs below. Then complete the exercise that follows.

Look for these signal words to help you compare and contrast.

- To show similar things: *like, the same as*

- To show different things: *different from, by contrast*

What's for Dinner?

Plants make their own food inside their leaves. Plants take in water and air from their environment. The leaves soak up sunlight. Plants use the Sun's energy to make food from water and a gas in the air. This food can be stored in roots, leaves, and other plant parts for use later on. . . . Living things that can make their own food are called **producers**. Plants are producers.

Since your body can't produce its own food, as a plant does, you have to get it another way—by eating something else. That means that you are a consumer. A **consumer** is a living thing that eats plants, animals, or other living things.

Make a chart like the one shown. Compare and contrast producers and consumers by completing your chart.

Producers	Consumers

Using MATH SKILLS

Using Math → Analyze Data

Some birds migrate very long distances. This table shows distances, in kilometers, that some birds migrate.

Migration Distances of Selected Birds	
Bird	**One-way Distance (km)**
Arctic tern	17,600
Atlantic brant	1,400
Barn swallow	9,600
Long-tailed jaeger	11,200
Pacific brant	4,000
Pacific golden plover	3,200
Snow goose	4,000
Whooping crane	4,800

Use the data in the table to complete the exercises.

1. Write the migration distances for these birds in order from shortest to longest.

2. Which of the birds listed migrates the longest distance? the shortest distance?

3. The arctic tern migrates for eight months each year. How many months is this bird not migrating?

4. How far does the whooping crane travel on a round-trip migration?

You may wish to use a calculator for Exercises 5 and 6.

5. How much longer is the round trip of the snow goose than the round trip of the Atlantic brant?

6. The Pacific brant migrates 4,000 km in three days. If the bird were to fly the same distance each day, how many kilometers would it fly in a day?

E79

UNIT E

WRAP-UP!

On your own, use scientific methods to investigate a question about roles of living things.

THINK LIKE A SCIENTIST

Ask a Question

Pose a question about roles of living things that you would like to investigate. For example, ask, "How does temperature affect the activity of decomposers?"

Make a Hypothesis

Suggest a hypothesis that is a possible answer to the question. One hypothesis is that a low temperature slows the activity of decomposers.

Plan and Do a Test

Plan a controlled experiment to compare the action of decomposers at different temperatures. You could start with two samples of moldy bread, self-sealing sandwich bags, and a refrigerator. Develop a procedure that uses these materials to test the hypothesis. With permission, carry out your experiment. Follow the safety guidelines on pages S14–S15.

Record and Analyze

Observe carefully and record your data accurately. Make repeated observations.

Draw Conclusions

Look for evidence to support the hypothesis or to show that it is false. Draw conclusions about the hypothesis. Repeat the experiment to verify the results.

WRITING IN SCIENCE
Outline

Write an outline for a report on animal or plant adaptations. Research the information for your outline. Follow these guidelines for your outline.

- Write a title for your outline.
- Put Roman numerals (I, II, III) next to main ideas.
- Put capital letters (A, B) next to supporting details.
- Include three main heads with two details for each.

E80

SCIENCE and MATH TOOLBOX

Using a Hand Lens

A hand lens is a tool that magnifies objects, or makes objects appear larger. This makes it possible for you to see details of an object that would be hard to see without the hand lens.

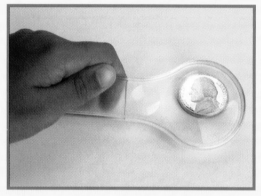

▲ Place the lens above the object.

▲ Move the lens slowly toward you.

Look at a Coin or a Stamp

1. Place an object such as a coin or a stamp on a table or other flat surface.

2. Hold the hand lens just above the object. As you look through the lens, slowly move the lens away from the object. Notice that the object appears to get larger.

3. Keep moving the lens until the object begins to look a little blurry. Then move the hand lens a little closer to the object until the object is once again in sharp focus.

If the object starts to look blurry, move the lens toward the object. ▶

Making a Bar Graph

A bar graph helps you organize and compare data.

Make a Bar Graph of Animal Heights

Animals come in all different shapes and sizes. You can use the information in the table to make a bar graph of animal heights.

Heights of Animals	
Animal	Height (cm)
Bear	240
Elephant	315
Cow	150
Giraffe	570
Camel	210
Horse	165

1. Draw the side and the bottom of the graph. Label the side of the graph as shown. The numbers will show the height of the animals in centimeters.

3. Choose a title for your graph. Your title should describe the subject of the graph.

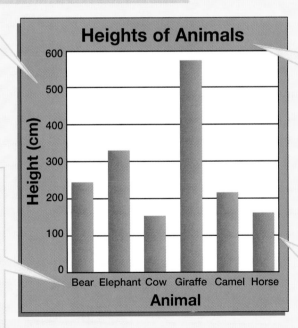

2. Label the bottom of the graph. Write the names of the animals at the bottom so that there is room to draw the bars.

4. Draw bars to show the height of each animal. Some heights are between two numbers.

Using a Calculator

After you've made measurements, a calculator can help you analyze your data.

Add and Multiply Decimals

Suppose you're an astronaut. You may take 8 pounds of Moon rocks back to Earth. The table shows the weights of the rocks. Can you take them all? Use a calculator to find out.

Weight of Moon Rocks	
Moon Rock	Weight of Rock on Moon (lb)
Rock 1	1.7
Rock 2	1.8
Rock 3	2.6
Rock 4	1.5

1. To add, press:

1 $.$ 7 $+$ 1 $.$ 8 $+$

2 $.$ 6 $+$ 1 $.$ 5 $=$

Display: 7.6

2. If you make a mistake, press the clear entry key (CE/C) once. Enter the number again. Then continue adding. (Note: If you press CE/C twice, it will clear all.)

3. Your total is 7.6 pounds. You can take the four Moon rocks back to Earth.

4. How much do the Moon rocks weigh on Earth? Objects weigh six times as much on Earth as they do on the Moon. You can use a calculator to multiply.

Press: 7 $.$ 6 $×$ 6 $=$

Display: 45.6

5. The rocks weigh 45.6 pounds on Earth.

clear entry

divide
multiply
plus
equal

Making a Tally Chart

A tally chart can help you keep track of items you are counting. Sometimes you need to count many different items. It may be hard to count all of the items of the same type as a group. That's when a tally chart can be helpful.

Make a Tally Chart of Birds Seen

These students are bird watchers. They're making a tally chart to record how many birds of each type they see.

Here are the tallies they have made so far.

Type of Bird	Tally
Cardinal	||
Blue jay	‖‖‖ ‖‖‖ ‖‖‖
Mockingbird	||||
Hummingbird	‖‖‖ ||
House sparrow	‖‖‖ ‖‖‖ ‖‖‖ ‖‖‖	
Robin	‖‖‖ ‖‖‖ ||

Every time you count one item, you make one tally.

When you reach five, draw the fifth tally as a line through the other four.

To find the total number of robins, count by fives and then ones.

You can use your tally chart to make a chart with numbers.

Type of Bird	Tally
Cardinal	2
Blue jay	15
Mockingbird	4
Hummingbird	7
House sparrow	21
Robin	12

What kind of bird was seen most often?

Now use a tally chart to record how many cars of different colors pass your school.

Using a Tape Measure or Ruler

Tape measures and rulers are tools for measuring the length of objects and distances. Scientists most often use units such as meters, centimeters, and millimeters when making length measurements.

Use a Tape Measure

1. Measure the distance around a jar. Wrap the tape around the jar.

2. Find the line where the tape begins to wrap over itself.

3. Record the distance around the jar to the nearest centimeter.

Use a Metric Ruler

1. Measure the length of your shoe. Place the ruler or the meterstick on the floor. Line up the end of the ruler with the heel of your shoe.

2. Notice where the other end of your shoe lines up with the ruler.

3. Look at the scale on the ruler. Record the length of your shoe to the nearest centimeter and to the nearest millimeter.

Measuring
Volume

A graduated cylinder, a measuring cup, and a beaker are used to measure volume. Volume is the amount of space something takes up. Most of the containers that scientists use to measure volume have a scale marked in milliliters (mL).

Measure the Volume of a Liquid

1. Measure the volume of juice. Pour some juice into a measuring container.

2. Move your head so that your eyes are level with the top of the juice. Read the scale line that is closest to the surface of the juice. If the surface of the juice is curved up on the sides, look at the lowest point of the curve.

3. Read the measurement on the scale. You can estimate the value between two lines on the scale.

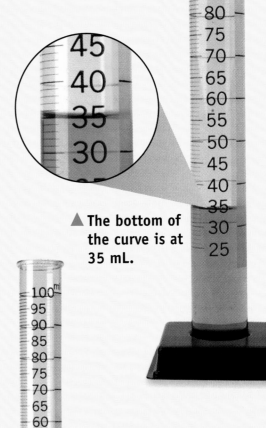

▲ The bottom of the curve is at 35 mL.

This beaker has marks for each 25 mL. ▶

This graduated cylinder has marks for every 1 mL. ▶

▲ This measuring cup has marks for each 25 mL.

Using a Thermometer

A thermometer is used to measure temperature. When the liquid in the tube of a thermometer gets warmer, it expands and moves farther up the tube. Different scales can be used to measure temperature, but scientists usually use the Celsius scale.

Measure the Temperature of a Cold Liquid

1. Take a chilled liquid out of the refrigerator. Half fill a cup with the liquid.

2. Hold the thermometer so that the bulb is in the center of the liquid. Be sure that there are no bright lights or direct sunlight shining on the bulb.

3. Wait a few minutes until you see the liquid in the tube of the thermometer stop moving. Read the scale line that is closest to the top of the liquid in the tube. The thermometer shown reads 21°C (about 70°F).

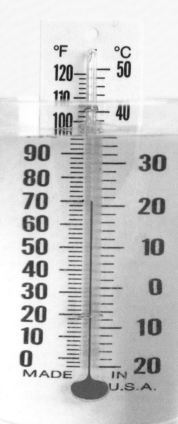

Using a Balance

A balance is used to measure mass. Mass is the amount of matter in an object. To find the mass of an object, place it in the left pan of the balance. Place standard masses in the right pan.

Measure the Mass of a Ball

1. Check that the empty pans are balanced, or level with each other. When balanced, the pointer on the base should be at the middle mark. If it needs to be adjusted, move the slider on the back of the balance a little to the left or right.

2. Place a ball on the left pan. Then add standard masses, one at a time, to the right pan. When the pointer is at the middle mark again, each pan holds the same amount of matter and has the same mass.

3. Add the numbers marked on the masses in the pan. The total is the mass of the ball in grams.

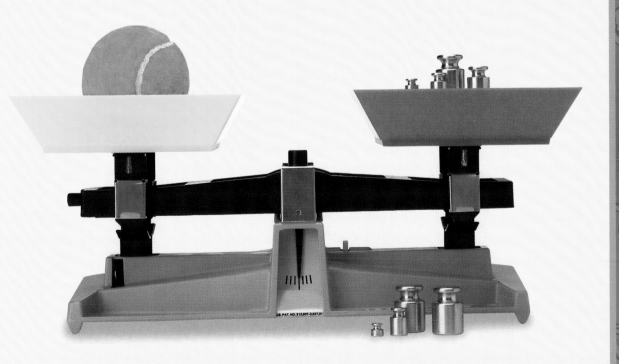

Making a Chart to Organize Data

A chart can help you keep track of information. When you organize information, or data, it is easier to read, compare, or classify it.

Classifying Animals

Suppose you are studying characteristics of different animals. You want to organize the data that you collect.

Look at the data below. To put this data in a chart, you could base the chart on the two characteristics listed— the number of wings and the number of legs.

My Data

Fleas have no wings. Fleas have six legs.

Snakes have no wings or legs.

A bee has four wings. It has six legs.

Spiders never have wings. They have eight legs.

A dog has no wings. It has four legs.

Birds have two wings and two legs.

A cow has no wings. It has four legs.

A butterfly has four wings. It has six legs.

Give the chart a title that describes the data in it.

Name categories, or groups, that describe the data you have collected.

Make sure the information is recorded correctly in each column.

Animals—Number of Wings and Legs

Animal	Number of Wings	Number of Legs
Flea	0	6
Snake	0	0
Bee	4	6
Spider	0	8
Dog	0	4
Bird	2	2
Cow	0	4
Butterfly	4	6

Next, you could make another chart to show animal classification based on number of legs only.

Reading a Circle Graph

A circle graph shows a whole divided into parts. You can use a circle graph to compare the parts to each other. You can also use it to compare the parts to the whole.

A Circle Graph of Fuel Use

This circle graph shows fuel use in the United States. The graph has 10 equal parts, or sections. Each section equals $\frac{1}{10}$ of the whole. One whole equals $\frac{10}{10}$.

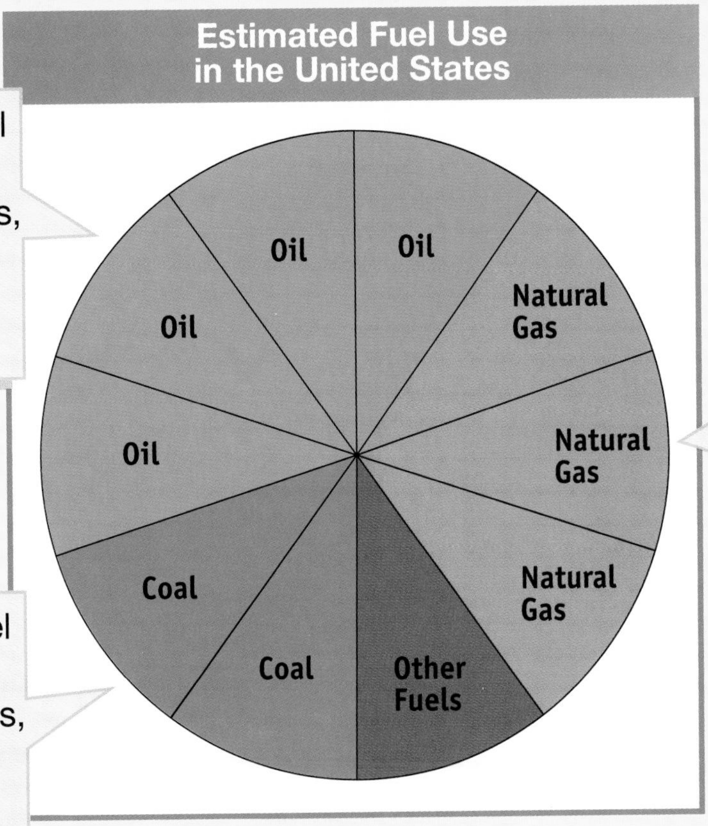

Estimated Fuel Use in the United States

Of all the fuel used in the United States, 4 out of 10 parts, or $\frac{4}{10}$, is oil.

Of all the fuel used in the United States, 3 out of 10 parts, or $\frac{3}{10}$, is natural gas.

Of all the fuel used in the United States, 2 out of 10 parts, or $\frac{2}{10}$, is coal.

Oil
Oil
Oil
Oil
Natural Gas
Natural Gas
Natural Gas
Coal
Coal
Other Fuels

Measuring
Elapsed Time

A calendar can help you find out how much time has passed, or elapsed, in days or weeks. A clock can help you see how much time has elapsed in hours and minutes. A clock with a second hand or a stopwatch can help you find out how many seconds have elapsed.

Using a Calendar to Find Elapsed Days

This is a calendar for the month of October. October has 31 days. Suppose it is October 22 and you begin an experiment. You need to check the experiment two days from the start date and one week from the start date. That means you would check it on Wednesday, October 24, and again on Monday, October 29. October 29 is 7 days after October 22.

Monday, Tuesday, Wednesday, Thursday, and Friday are weekdays. Saturday and Sunday are weekends.

Last month ended on Sunday, September 30.

October

Sunday	Monday	Tuesday	Wednesday	Thursday	Friday	Saturday
	1	2	3	4	5	6
7	8	9	10	11	12	13
14	15	16	17	18	19	20
21	22	23	24	25	26	27
28	29	30	31			

Next month begins on Thursday, November 1.

Using a Clock or a Stopwatch to Find Elapsed Time

You need to time an experiment for 20 minutes.

It is 1:30 P.M.

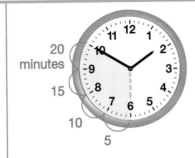

Stop at 1:50 P.M.

You need to time an experiment for 15 seconds. You can use the second hand of a clock or watch.

60 seconds = 1 minute

Start the experiment when the second hand is on number 6.

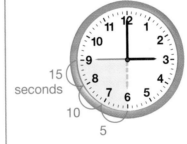

Stop when 15 seconds have passed and the second hand is on the 9.

You can use a stopwatch.

Press the reset button on a stopwatch so that you see 0:00oo.

Press the start button. When you see 0:15oo, press the stop button.

MEASUREMENTS

Volume
1 L of sports drink is a little more than 1 qt.

Area
A basketball court covers about 4,700 ft². It covers about 435 m².

Mass and Weight
A basketball has a mass of about 650 g. It weighs about $1\frac{1}{2}$ lb.

Metric Measures

Temperature
Ice melts at 0 degrees Celsius (°C)

Water freezes at 0°C

Water boils at 100°C

Length and Distance
1,000 meters (m) = 1 kilometer (km)

100 centimeters (cm) = 1 m

10 millimeters (mm) = 1 cm

Force
1 newton (N) =
   1 kilogram x meter/second/second
   (kg x m/s²)

Volume
1 cubic meter (m³) = 1 m x 1 m x 1 m

1 cubic centimeter (cm³) =
   1 cm x 1 cm x 1 cm

1 liter (L) = 1,000 milliliters (mL)

1 cm³ = 1 mL

Area
1 square kilometer (km²) = 1 km x 1 km

1 hectare = 10,000 m²

Mass
1,000 grams (g) = 1 kilogram (kg)

1,000 milligrams (mg) = 1 g

Temperature
The temperature at an indoor basketball game might be 25°C, which is 77°F.

Length/ Distance
A basketball rim is about 10 ft high, or a little more than 3 m from the floor.

Customary Measures

Temperature
Ice melts at 32 degrees Fahrenheit (°F)
Water freezes at 32°F
Water boils at 212°F

Length and Distance
12 inches (in.) = 1 foot (ft)
3 ft = 1 yard (yd)
5,280 ft = 1 mile (mi)

Weight
16 ounces (oz) = 1 pound (lb)
2,000 pounds = 1 ton (T)

Volume of Fluids
8 fluid ounces (fl oz) = 1 cup (c)
2 c = 1 pint (pt)
2 pt = 1 quart (qt)
4 qt = 1 gallon (gal)

Metric and Customary Rates
km/h = kilometers per hour
m/s = meters per second
mph = miles per hour

GLOSSARY

Pronunciation Key

Symbol	Key Words
a	c**a**t
ā	**a**pe
ä	c**o**t, c**a**r
e	t**e**n, b**e**rry
ē	m**e**
i	f**i**t, h**e**re
ī	**i**ce, f**i**re
ō	g**o**
ô	f**a**ll, f**o**r
oi	**oi**l
o͞o	l**oo**k, p**u**ll
o͞o	t**oo**l, r**u**le
ou	**ou**t, cr**ow**d
u	**u**p
ʉ	f**u**r, sh**i**rt
ə	**a** in **a**go
	e in ag**e**nt
	i in penc**i**l
	o in at**o**m
	u in circ**u**s
b	**b**ed
d	**d**og
f	**f**all

Symbol	Key Words
g	**g**et
h	**h**elp
j	**j**ump
k	**k**iss, **c**all
l	**l**eg
m	**m**eat
n	**n**ose
p	**p**ut
r	**r**ed
s	**s**ee
t	**t**op
v	**v**at
w	**w**ish
y	**y**ard
z	**z**ebra
ch	**ch**in, ar**ch**
ŋ	ri**ng**, dri**n**k
sh	**sh**e, pu**sh**
th	**th**in, tru**th**
th	**th**en, fa**th**er
zh	mea**s**ure

A heavy stress mark (′) is placed after a syllable that gets a heavy, or primary, stress, as in **picture** (pik′chər).

A

acid rain (as'id rān) Rain that contains a large amount of acids, and that results from the burning of fossil fuels. (D43) *Acid rain* can harm living things.

adaptation (ad əp tā'shən) Behavior or part of a living thing that helps it survive in a certain environment. (A28, E40) A rose's thorns and a camel's hump are *adaptations*.

adult (ə dult') The last stage of a life cycle. (A23) The butterfly is the *adult* stage of a caterpillar.

air pollution (er pə lōō'shən) Any harmful or unclean materials in the air. (D17) Burning fuels can cause *air pollution*.

aquifer (ak'wə fər) An underground layer of rock where ground water collects. (D31) The water in a well usually comes from an *aquifer*.

astronomer (ə strän'ə mər) A scientist who studies the origin, features, and motion of objects in space. (B14) *Astronomers* use telescopes, cameras, and space probes to study the stars.

atmosphere (at'məs fir) The layer of gases surrounding Earth or another planet. (B12, D8) Earth's *atmosphere* is made up of gases such as oxygen, nitrogen, and carbon dioxide.

atom (at'əm) The smallest particle of matter. (C20) Water is made up of the *atoms* of two different substances—hydrogen and oxygen.

axis (ak'sis) The imaginary line on which an object rotates. (B38) Earth's *axis* runs between the North Pole and the South Pole.

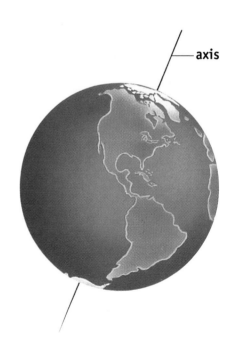

axis

behavior (bē hāv′yər) The way an animal typically acts in a certain situation. (E42) One *behavior* of pill bugs is to move toward moist, dark places.

camouflage (kam′ə fläzh) The ability to blend in with the surroundings. (E45) An animal's fur or skin can be *camouflage*, helping the animal hunt or avoid hunters.

carnivore (kär′nə vôr) An animal that *eats* only other animals. (E17) Wolves, cougars, lions, hawks, and owls are *carnivores*.

chemical change (kem′i kəl chānj) A change in matter in which different kinds of matter are formed. (C23) A *chemical change* occurs when wood burns and becomes gases and ash.

chemical property (kem′i kəl präp′ər tē) A description of how matter can change into another kind of matter. (C14) A *chemical property* of paper is its ability to burn.

community (kə myōō′nə tē) A group of plants and animals that live in a certain area and depend on one another. (E31) A pond's plants and animals form a *community*.

complete metamorphosis (kəm plēt′ met ə môr′fə sis) The four-stage life cycle of many insects. (A23) A life cycle that goes from egg to larva to pupa to adult is described as a *complete metamorphosis*.

compound machine (kam-pound mə shēn′) A machine that is made up of two or more simple machines. (C76) A pair of scissors is a *compound machine* because it contains two kinds of simple machines—a lever and a wedge.

condense (kən dens') To change form from a gas to a liquid. (C55, D29) When water vapor in the air cools, it *condenses* into tiny droplets of liquid water.

conduction (kən duk'shən) The movement of heat by direct contact between particles of matter. (C47) Heat moves by *conduction* from warmer matter with faster-moving particles to cooler matter with slower-moving particles.

conductor (kən duk'tər) A material that transfers heat or electricity easily. (C48) Metals are good *conductors* of heat.

cone (kōn) The part of a conifer that produces pollen or seeds. (A50) Each *cone* is a woody stalk covered with stiff scales.

constellation (kän stə lā'shən) A group of stars that form a pattern that looks like a person, animal, or object. (B46) Different *constellations* are visible from Earth at different times of year.

consumer (kən soom'ər) A living thing that eats other living things to survive. (E17) Animals are *consumers*.

controlled experiment (kən-trōld' ek sper'ə mənt) A test of a hypothesis in which the setups are identical in all ways except one. (S7) In the *controlled experiment*, one beaker of water contained salt; all the other beakers contained only water.

convection (kən vek'shən) The circulation of heat through a liquid or gas (fluid) by the movements of particles from one part of the matter to another. (C48) *Convection* takes place in a room with a heater: As hot air rises from the heater, cool air flows down to take its place.

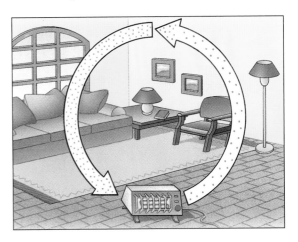

crater (krāt'ər) A bowl-shaped pit. (B11) *Craters* on the Moon and on Earth were formed by meteorites striking the surface.

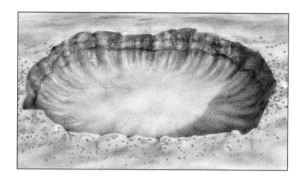

---D---

decomposer (dē kəm pōz'ər) A living thing that breaks down and feeds on the remains of once-living things. (E18) *Decomposers* such as mushrooms recycle the remains of once-living things.

dormancy (dôr'mən sē) A decrease in plant activity during the winter. (E76) Sap flows in maple trees in the spring after the tree's *dormancy* during winter.

---E---

earthquake (ʉrth'kwāk) A sudden movement of large sections of rock beneath Earth's surface. (D51) Books tumbled from shelves during the *earthquake*.

ecosystem (ek'ō sis təm) A place where living and nonliving things interact. (E64) The animals, plants, and insects in the tops of trees in a rain forest have their own *ecosystem*.

egg (eg) The first stage in the life cycle of almost all animals. (A14) Birds hatch from *eggs* outside the mother bird's body.

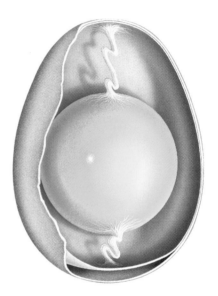

embryo (em'brē ō) An animal or plant in the earliest stages of its development. (A15, A39) A plant *embryo* is the tiny plant that is found inside a seed.

energy (en'ər jē) The ability to cause a change in matter. (C31) A car uses *energy* from gasoline or diesel fuel to run.

energy of motion (en'ər jē uv mō'shən) The energy that moving matter has. (C31) Sliding downhill on a sled, tossing a basketball into the air, and flying a kite in the wind are examples of *energy of motion*.

environment (en vī'rən mənt) All the surrounding living and nonliving things that affect a living thing. (E10) A drop of water, a rotting log, a desert, an ocean, and a rain forest are examples of different *environments*.

equator (ē kwāt'ər) An imaginary line that circles Earth halfway between the two poles. (B64) If you live near the *equator*, you live in a hot climate because your region receives direct sunlight most of the time.

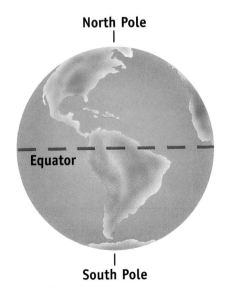

North Pole

Equator

South Pole

erosion (ē rō'zhən) The breaking up and moving of weathered rocks from one place to another. (D52) The Grand Canyon was formed by millions of years of *erosion*.

evaporate (ē vap'ə rāt) To change form from a liquid to a gas. (C54, D29) On a warm dry day, puddles on the sidewalk *evaporate* quickly.

extinction (ek stiŋk'shən) The permanent disappearance of all living things of a certain kind. (E20) The *extinction* of the saber-toothed cat is a mystery that some scientists are working to solve.

flare (fler) A bright area on the surface of the Sun caused by a solar storm. (B27) A solar *flare* is hotter than surrounding areas of the Sun and so is brighter.

food chain (fōōd chān) The path that energy takes through a community as one living thing eats another. (E26) The first link in a *food chain* is usually a plant.

food web (fōōd web) Two or more food chains that overlap and link. (E28) A *food web* connects animals through the plants and animals that they eat.

force (fôrs) A push or a pull. (C64) When you open a door, you apply a *force*.

fossil fuel (fäs′əl fyōō′əl) A fuel formed over time from the remains of plants or animals. (D10) *Fossil fuels* such as oil, coal, and natural gas are found underground.

freeze (frēz) To change form from a liquid to a solid. (C55) The loss of heat causes a liquid to *freeze*.

friction (frik′shən) A force that makes it hard for two objects to move past one another easily when the objects touch. (C46) *Friction* causes your hands to get warm when you rub them together.

fruit (frōōt) The part of a flower that forms around a seed. (A45) Cucumbers, tomatoes, oranges, peaches, and pears are *fruits*.

fulcrum (ful′krəm) The fixed point around which a lever turns. (C73) If you use a lever to lift an object, the *fulcrum* is located between you and the object you are lifting.

gas (gas) A state of matter that has no definite shape and does not take up a definite amount of space. (C20) A *gas* spreads out evenly to fill whatever space it is in.

germ (jʉrm) A tiny organism that can cause disease. (D37) Chlorine kills some of the *germs* in water.

germinate (jʉr′mə nāt) To sprout and begin to develop into a seedling. (A40) Most kinds of seeds need moisture, air, and warmth to *germinate*.

glacier (glā′shər) A large mass of slow-moving ice. (D53) When a *glacier* meets the sea, large chunks of ice fall off, forming icebergs.

gravity (grav′i tē) A force that pulls two or more objects toward each other. (B22, C65) To fly into space, a rocket must overcome Earth's *gravity*.

ground water (ground wôt′ər) The water found beneath Earth's surface. (D31) In some areas, *ground water* fills the small spaces that are between underground rocks, soil, and sand.

habitat (hab′i tat) The place where an animal or a plant lives. (E10) Deer live in a woodland *habitat*.

heat (hēt) The energy of moving particles of matter. (C32) Adding *heat* to matter causes its particles to move faster.

herbivore (hʉr′bə vôr) An animal that eats only plants. (E18) Cows and rabbits are *herbivores*.

hibernation (hī bər nā′shən) A deep sleep that helps some animals survive the winter. (E75) An animal that is in *hibernation* breathes slowly, has a slow heartbeat, and has a low body temperature.

hypothesis (hī päth′ə sis) An idea about or explanation of how or why something happens. (S6) The *hypothesis* that the Earth revolves around the Sun has been supported by evidence gathered by astronomers.

inclined plane (in klīnd′ plān) A simple machine with a slanted surface. It allows objects to be raised or lowered from one level to another without lifting them. (C74) A ramp is a kind of *inclined plane*.

incomplete metamorphosis
(in kəm plēt′ met ə môr′fə sis)
The three-stage life cycle of some
insects. (A24) A life cycle that goes
from egg to nymph to adult is
called *incomplete metamorphosis*.

inexhaustible resource (in eg-
zôs′tə bəl rē′sôrs) A natural
resource that does not decrease, or
become used up, as people use it.
(D11) Wind can't be used up so it
is an *inexhaustible resource*.

insulator (in′sə lāt ər) A poor
conductor of heat or electricity.
(C48) Air that is trapped in the
small spaces between fibers of
clothing acts as an *insulator*.

larva (lär′və) The second stage
in the life cycle of an insect that
undergoes complete
metamorphosis. (A23) A butterfly
larva is called a caterpillar.

lava (lä′və) Liquid rock flowing
on the surface. (D51) Fires broke
out when *lava* reached the wooden
frames of houses.

lever (lev′ər) A simple machine
made up of a bar that turns, or
rotates, around a fixed point. (C73)
A *lever* helps to lift a heavy object
or a tight lid with less effort.

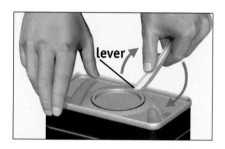

life cycle (līf sī′kəl) The
ordered changes that occur during
the lifetime of a living thing. (A9)
An insect goes through three or
four stages in its *life cycle*.

liquid (lik′wid) A state of matter
that has no definite shape but
takes up a definite amount of
space. (C20) At room temperature,
water is a *liquid*.

lunar eclipse (lo͞o′nər i klips′)
The darkening of the Moon when
it moves into Earth's shadow.
(B76) During a *lunar eclipse*,
Earth blocks the Sun's light from
reaching the Moon directly.

machine (mə shēn′) Something that makes a task easy to do by reducing the amount of force needed to do a job. (C72) A *machine* can make it easier to move, lift, carry, or cut something.

magma (mag′mə) Liquid rock deep inside Earth. (D50) After *magma* flows out of a volcano the magma is called lava.

mass (mas) The amount of matter that something contains. (C10) An elephant has more *mass* than an insect.

matter (mat′ər) Anything that has mass and takes up space. (C10) Every living and nonliving thing around you is made of *matter*.

melt (melt) To change form from a solid to a liquid. (C54) Ice *melts* at 0°C (32°F) and iron melts at 1,530°C (2,786°F).

meteorite (mēt′ē ər īt) A chunk of rock or metal that has fallen from space. (B11) A *meteorite* may be as small as a grain of sand or as large as a house.

migrate (mī′grāt) To move to another region as the seasons change. (E74) Many northern birds and butterflies *migrate* south during the winter.

minerals (min′ər əlz) Solids found in nature that have a definite chemical makeup. (D10) Calcium is a *mineral* found in milk and cheese.

natural resource (nach′ər əl rē′sôrs) A material found in or on Earth that people use. (D9) *Natural resources* include water, minerals, fossil fuels, soil, plants, and animals.

nonrenewable resource (nän ri no͞o′ə bəl rē′sôrs) A natural resource that cannot be replaced within a person's lifetime. (D11) Diamonds are *nonrenewable resources* because it will take nature millions of years to make more.

nutrient (nōō′trē ənt) Any substance used by living things for energy, growth, repair, or other life processes. (E43) Proteins, carbohydrates, and fats are *nutrients* found in food.

nymph (nimf) The second stage in the life cycle of an insect undergoing incomplete metamorphosis. (A24) A grasshopper *nymph* looks similar to a small adult.

omnivore (äm′ni vôr) An animal that eats both plants and animals. (E18) Because bears will eat both berries and fish, bears are classified as *omnivores*.

opaque (ō pāk′) Materials that block light. (C35) *Opaque* curtains are used in theaters to block the light from windows.

orbit (ôr′bit) The path a planet, moon, or other object takes around another. (B46) The Moon is seen in different phases as it moves through its *orbit* around Earth.

parasite (par′ə sīt) A living thing that, at some point in its life, lives on or in another living thing and harms it. (E52) Fleas, lice, and some kinds of worms are *parasites*.

petal (pet′′l) The brightly colored part of a flower that helps attract birds, bees, and other insects to the flower. (A44) A *petal* is one of the three main parts of a flower.

phase (fāz) Any stage in the series of changes in the apparent shape of the Moon. (B53) The Moon's shape appears to change with each *phase*.

physical change (fiz′i kəl chānj) A change in the size, shape, or state of matter. (C23) When water freezes, it undergoes a *physical change* from a liquid to a solid.

physical property (fiz′i kəl präp′ ər tē) A quality of matter that can be measured or observed with the senses without changing the matter into another kind of matter. (C14) A *physical property* of ice is its hardness.

pistil (pis′til) The central part in a flower where seeds form. (A44) For seeds to form in a plant, the pollen must travel to the *pistil*.

planet (plan′it) A large body that orbits a star and does not produce light of its own. (B47) Earth is a *planet*.

pollen (päl′ən) The powdery grains in a flower; they must be carried from a stamen to a pistil in order for seeds to form. (A44) Bees move *pollen* from one flower to another.

pollination (päl ə nā′shən) The process by which pollen reaches a pistil. (A44) After *pollination*, a flower can produce seeds.

pollution (pə lōō′shən) Any unwanted or harmful material found in the environment. (D17) Air *pollution* can cause damage to your lungs.

precipitation (prē sip ə tā′shən) The liquid or solid forms of water that fall to Earth. (D31) Rain, sleet, hail, and snow are different kinds of *precipitation*.

predator (pred′ə tər) An animal that hunts other animals for food. (E27) Hawks, cougars, and sharks are *predators*.

prey (prā) An animal hunted for food by another animal. (E27) Rabbits, mice, small fish, and insects are often *prey* for larger animals.

producer (prō dōōs′ər) A living thing that can make its own food. (E16) Plants, such as trees and grass, are *producers*.

prominence (präm′ə nəns) A huge loop of gas that appears on the edge of the Sun. (B27) *Prominences* are caused by magnetic storms on the Sun.

property (präp'ər tē) Something that describes matter. (C12) A *property* of water in its liquid form is its ability to flow.

pulley (pool'ē) A wheel around which a rope or chain is passed. (C75) A *pulley* helps lift objects that would be too heavy to lift directly.

pupa (pyoo'pə) The third stage in the life cycle of an insect undergoing complete metamorphosis. (A23) As a *pupa*, an insect is enclosed in a cocoon, or case.

radiation (rā dē ā'shən) The movement of heat energy in the form of waves. (C49) Heat from a campfire reaches you through *radiation*.

renewable resource (ri noo'ə-bəl rē'sôrs) A natural resource that can be replaced within a person's lifetime. (D11) Lumber is a *renewable resource* if new trees are planted to replace cut trees.

reservoir (rez'ər vwär) The body of water that is stored behind a dam. (D31) A *reservoir* stores fresh water for a town or city.

revolve (ri välv') To move in a circle or orbit. (B46) Earth *revolves* around the Sun.

rotation (rō tā'shən) The spinning motion around an axis. (B38) Earth takes 24 hours to complete one *rotation*.

scale (skāl) A cone's woody part on which seeds grow. (A51) A pine cone's *scales* protect its seeds.

season (sē'zən) Any of the four parts of the year. (B65) The four *seasons* are spring, summer, fall, and winter.

seed coat (sēd kōt) The part of a seed that protects the plant embryo. (A39) The *seed coat* of a coconut is hard, thick, and brown.

seedling (sēd'liŋ) The new plant that develops from an embryo and has roots, a stem, and leaves. (A41) A tomato *seedling* can be started indoors in early spring and planted outside in May.

simple machine (sim′pəl mə shēn′) A device that changes the size or direction of a force. (C73) A lever is a *simple machine*.

soil The loose material that covers much of Earth's surface. (D56) As they grow, most plants extend their roots into *soil*.

solar eclipse (sō′lər i klips′) The blocking of light from the Sun when the Moon moves between it and Earth. (B75) During a *solar eclipse*, the Sun's light is blocked by the Moon.

solar energy (sō′lər en′ər jē) Energy produced by the Sun. (C36) *Solar energy* can be used to produce electricity.

solar system (sō′lər sis′təm) The Sun and all the planets and other objects that orbit it. (B47) Earth is one of nine planets in the *solar system*.

solid (säl′id) A state of matter that has a definite shape and takes up a definite amount of space. (C19, D14) A rock, a piece of ice, and a chair are all examples of *solids*.

species (spē′shēz) A group of living things that can produce living things of the same kind. (A10) The lion *species* cannot produce young of the gorilla *species*.

stamen (stā′mən) The part of a flower that produces pollen, which is needed to form seeds. (A44) *Stamens* are often long and have a fuzzy end.

star (stär) A ball of very hot gases that gives off light and other energy. (B27) The Sun is a *star*.

states of matter (stāts uv mat′r.) The three forms that matter takes—solid, liquid, and gas. (C19) Water exists naturally in all three *states of matter*.

stored energy (stôrd en′ər jē) Energy in matter that can cause matter to move or change. (C31) Fuels have *stored energy* from the Sun.

sunspot (sun′spöt) A dark area on the surface of the Sun, caused by a solar storm. (B27) A *sunspot* appears darker because it is cooler than surrounding areas of the Sun.

surface water (sʉr′fis wôt′ər) Fresh water in lakes, streams, and rivers. (D30) People often pipe *surface water* to nearby cities.

telescope (tel'ə skōp) A device that makes distant objects appear larger and brighter. (B15) A *telescope* is used to study stars and other planets.

temperature (tem'pər ə chər) A measure of how hot or cold something is. (C45) *Temperature* is measured with a thermometer.

theory (thē'ə rē) A hypothesis that is supported by a lot of evidence and is widely accepted by scientists. (S9) The big-bang *theory* offers an explanation for the origin of the universe.

topsoil (täp' soil) A mixture of weathered rock and humus (decayed plant and animal matter). (D57) *Topsoil* contains nutrients that help plants to grow.

variable (ver'ē ə bəl) The one difference in the setups of a controlled experiment; provides a comparison for testing a hypothesis. (S7) The *variable* in an experiment with plants was the amount of water given each plant.

volcano (väl kā'nō) An opening in the ground through which hot ash, gases, and lava move from inside Earth to the surface, sometimes forming a cone-shaped hill or mountain. (D51) Lava poured out of the *volcano,* adding a new layer of rock to the land.

volume (väl yo͞om) The amount of space that matter takes up. (C11) A *volume* of water that measures a pint weighs about a pound.

water cycle (wôt'ər sī'kəl) The path that water follows as it evaporates into the air, condenses into clouds, and returns to Earth as rain, snow, sleet, or hail. (D30) In the *water cycle*, water evaporates from lakes and oceans into the air, and then condenses and falls back to Earth as rain or snow.

water vapor (wôt'ər vā'pər) Water that is in the form of a gas. (D29) Steam, which is invisible, is *water vapor*.

weathering (we*th*'ər iŋ) The breaking up or wearing away of rocks. (D52) Rock formations in Arches National Park have been formed by the *weathering* action of wind and rain.

wetlands (wet'landz) Swamps, marshes, and bogs that are home to many kinds of animals and plants. (E65) *Wetlands* are low-lying areas where water is absorbed into underground aquifers.

wheel and axle (hwēl ənd ak'səl) A simple machine that is made up of two wheels that turn together. (C75) A doorknob, along with its shaft, is an example of a *wheel and axle*.

INDEX

* **Activity**

* Activity

CREDITS

ILLUSTRATORS
Cover: Garry Colby.

Think Like a Scientist: 4–6, 8–9: Garry Colby. 14: Laurie Hamilton. *Borders:* Garry Colby.

Unit A: 8–9: Kathy Rusynyk. 10–11: Steve McInterf. 14–15: A.J. Miller. 22: Doreen Gay Kasssel. 28–29: Adam Mathews. 38: Eldon Doty. 39: *t.* Ka Botzis, *b.* Rebeca Mereles. 44–45: Lori Anzalone. 47, 50, 52: Dan McGowan. 54: Paul Blakey. 58: Julie Carpenter. 61: Lori Anzalone.

Unit B: 7: Richard Courtney. 10: Randy Hamblin. 12–13: Richard Courtney. 14: Stephen Wagner. 20: Jenny Campbell. 21: A.J. Miller. 22: Jenny Campbell. 22: Robert Roper. 23: Jenny Campbell. 27: Richard Courtney. 28: David Barber. 29–31: Richard Courtney. 37: Tom Powers. 39: Verlin Miller. 40: Tom Powers. 42–43: Skip Baker. 44–45: Tom Powers. 46–47: Dennis Davidson. 48–49: Eldon Doty. 51–52, 54: Tim Blough. 55–56: Susan Simon. 57: Tom Powers. 64–65: Liz Conrad. 64–66: Uldis Klavins. 68–69: Jean and Mou-Sien Tseng. 70: Eureka Cartography. 70–71: Traci Harmon. 74–75: Jean and Mou-Sien Tseng. 76: Dennis Davidson. 77: Uldis Klavins.

Unit C: 15, 19–21: Andrew Shiff. 20, 25: Patrick Gnan. 26–27: Susan Simon. 28: Scott Luke. 30–33: Larry Jost. 34–35: Garry Colby. 36: Leslie Wolf. 44–46: Akio Matsuyoshi. 47: A.J. Miller. 49: Robert Roper. 50–51: Randy Hamblin. 54–56: Jim Turgeon. 57: Patrick Gnan. 64–65: Stephen Peringer. 66–67: Eldon Doty. 72: Patrick Gnan. 74: Jeff Stock. 75, 77: Patrick Gnan.

Unit D: 11: Eldon Doty. 14–15: Tim Blough. 16: Mike Kline. 17–18: Tim Blough. 25–27: Bob Brugger. 28: Mike Meaker. 30–31: Stephen Wagner. 31: Dan Clyne. 32–33: Robert Roper. 37: Stephen Bauer. 40–41: Eldon Doty. 42–43: Tom Pansini. 44: Robert Schuster. 45: Tom Pansini. 50: John Youssi. 59: Jeannie Winston. 60: Don Baker.

Unit E: 11–12: Higgins Bond. 16–19: Jim Owens. 20–21: Jeffrey Terreson. 26–27: Jenny Campbell. 27: Jackie Geyer. 28–29: Jenny Campbell. 30: Sarah Jane English. 32–33: Jim Salvati. 35: Jackie Geyer. 44–45: Phil Wilson. 48–53: Jenny Campbell. 54–56: Sarah Jane English. 55: Susan Melrath. 61: Jackie Geyer. 62–63: Deborah Pinkney. 64: Jackie Geyer. 66–67: Eldon Doty. 70–71: Tina Fong. 74–75: Robert Schuster. 77: Deborah Pinkney.

Math and Science Toolbox: *Logos:* Nancy Tobin. 14–15: Andrew Shiff. *Borders:* Garry Colby.

Glossary: 17–18: Richard Courtney. 19: *b.l.* Dan McGowan. *b.r.* Robert Roper. 20: *t.l.* Richard Courtney. *m.r.* A.J. Miller. 21: *m.l.* Liz Conrad. *m.r.* Jeffrey Terreson. 22–23: Stephen Wagoner. 24: Patrick Gnan. 25: Scott Ross. 26: Denise Davidson. 27: Stephen Wagoner. 28: Pat Gnan. 29 Denise Davidson. 30: *t.l.* Stephen Wagoner. *b.r.* Brad Gaber. 31: Stephen Wagoner.

PHOTOGRAPHS
All photographs by Houghton Mifflin Co. (HMCo.) unless otherwise noted.

Front Cover: *t.* Randy Ury/The Stock Market; *m.l.* A & L Sinbaldi/Tony Stone Images; *b.l.* Gary Vestal/Tony Stone Images; *b.r.* Superstock.

Think Like A Scientist: 4–5: Luiz Claudio Marigo/Peter Arnold, Inc.

Table of Contents: xiv: *l.* © James Steinberg/Photo Researchers, Inc.; *m.* © Gary Retherford/Photo Researchers, Inc.; *r.* Zig Leszczynski/Animals Animals/Earth Scenes.

Unit A 1: © Fletcher & Baylis/Photo Researchers, Inc. 2–3: *bkgd* © Fletcher & Baylis/Photo Researchers, Inc.; *inset* © J. Zerschling/Photo Researchers, Inc. 4–5: *bkgd.* Fred Hirschmann; *inset* Erik Hill/Anchorage Daily News. 8: *l.* Dwight R. Kuhn; *r.* Dwight R. Kuhn. 14: E.R. Degginger/Color-Pic, Inc. 16: *t.* E.R. Degginger/Color-Pic, Inc.; *b.* Frans Lanting/Minden Pictures. 17: *l.* Chick Master Incubator Company; *r.* Gil Taylor/Chick Master Incubator Company. 18: *t.* Hans & Judy Beste/Animals Animals/Earth Scenes; *b.r.* © M. Reardon/Photo Researchers, Inc.

19: *t.* Miriam Austerman/Animals Animals/Earth Scenes; *b.l.* Michio Hoshino/Minden Pictures; *b.r.* Frans Lanting/Minden Pictures. 22: *t.l.* Courtesy, Evelyn O'Shea; *t.r.* Courtesy, Evelyn O'Shea; *b.l.* Courtesy, Evelyn O'Shea; *b.r.* Courtesy, Evelyn O'Shea. 23: *t.l.* E.R. Degginger/Animals Animals/Earth Scenes; *t.r.* Patti Murray/Animals Animals/Earth Scenes; *b.l.* Patti Murray/Animals Animals/Earth Scenes; *b.r.* Patti Murray/Animals Animals/Earth Scenes. 25: *t.l.* Raymond A. Mendez/Animals Animals/Earth Scenes; *t.r.* John Pontier/Animals Animals/Earth Scenes. *b.* © David & Hayes Norris/Photo Researchers, Inc. 28: *l.* Anne Heimann; *r.* Anne Heimann. 29: *l.* Anne Heimann; *r.* Trevor Barrett/Animals Animals/Earth Scenes. 30–31: Flip Nicklin/Minden Pictures. 31: Jeff Foott/DRK Photo. 32: *l.* Michio Hoshino/Minden Pictures; *r.* Michio Hoshino/Minden Pictures. 34: © 1994 Jill Krementz. 34–35: *bkgd.* Antonio M. Rosario/The Image Bank. 40: *t.* S. Nielsen/Imagery; *m.* Runk/Schoenberger/Grant Heilman Photography, Inc.; *b.* E.R. Degginger/Color-Pic, Inc. 41: Dwight R. Kuhn. 46: *l.* Superstock; *r.* Superstock. 48: *t.* Grant Huntington for HMCo.; *m.* Grant Huntington for HMCo.; *b.* Grant Huntington for HMCo. 49: *t.r.* E.R. Degginger/Color-Pic, Inc.; *m.* E.R. Degginger/Color-Pic, Inc.; *b.l.* Grant Huntington for HMCo.; *b.r.* E.R. Degginger/Color-Pic, Inc. 53: *t.l.* David Austen/Tony Stone Images; *t.r.* David Austen/Animals Animals/Earth Scenes; *b.* Don Pitcher/Stock Boston. 55: Grant Huntington for HMCo. 56: Grant Huntington for HMCo. 57: *t.* Grant Huntington for HMCo.; *b.* Grant Huntington for HMCo. 58–59: Barry L. Runk/Grant Heilman Photography, Inc. 59: *t.* Runk/Schoenberger/Grant Heilman Photography, Inc. 60: *l.* Runk/Schoenberger/Grant Heilman Photography, Inc.; *r.* Jim Strauser/Grant Heilman Photography, Inc.

Unit B 1: UPI/Corbis Corporation. 2–3: UPI/Corbis Corporation. 4–5: *inset* Victor Aleman/2 Mun-Dos Communications. 11: *l.* NASA; *r.* H.R. Bramaz/Peter Arnold, Inc. 12: NASA/The Stock Market. 13: NASA. 15: *bkgd.* Corbis Corporation; *inset* Frank Rossotto/The Stock Market. 16: *t.* Photri, Inc. 17: NASA. 18: Grant Huntington for HMCo. 19: Grant Huntington for HMCo. 23: *l.* NASA; *r.* © NASA/Science Source/Photo Researchers, Inc. 24: Grant Huntington for HMCo. 25: Grant Huntington for HMCo. 26: Grant Huntington for HMCo. 29: *t.* Photri, Inc.; *b.* © Pekka Parviainen/Science Photo Library/Photo Researchers, Inc. 30: *l.* National Solar Observatory/Sacramento Peak; *r.* NASA/Frank P. Rossotto/Stocktrek. 32–33: E.R. Degginger/Color-Pic, Inc. 34: Grant Huntington for HMCo. 35: *t.* Grant Huntington for HMCo.; *b.* E.R. Degginger/Color-Pic, Inc. 37: *l.* Grant Huntington for HMCo.; *m.* Grant Huntington for HMCo. 38: © Sylvain Grandadam/Photo Researchers, Inc. 40: Dennis Cox/ChinaStock. 40–41: Oddo & Sinibaldi/The Stock Market. 41: *l.* Robert Holmes; *m.* D & J McClurg/Bruce Coleman Incorporated; *r.* Norman Owen Tomalin/Bruce Coleman Incorporated. 52: NASA. 58–59: *bkgd.* John Gerlach/Tom Stack & Associates; *inset* Doranne Jacobson. 62: *t.* Ken Karp for HMCo.; *b.* Ken Karp for HMCo. 63: Ken Karp for HMCo. 67: *bkgd.* Tibor Bognar/The Stock Market; *l. inset* Robert Frerck/Odyssey Productions; *r. inset* D. Donne Bryant. 68: Superstock. 69: *t.* Courtesy, National Maritime Museum. 70: *r.* Superstock. 71: Brian Stablyk/Tony Stone Images. 72: *t.* Ken Karp for HMCo.; *b.* George Post. 73: *t.* Ken Karp for HMCo.; *b.* S.Nielsen/Imagery. 74: Sen Sakamonto/Black Star.

Unit C 1: Adam Woolfitt/Corbis Corporation; 4–5: *bkgd.* G. Bliss/Masterfile Corporation; *inset* Stewart Cohen/Tony Stone Images. 23: *t.* Joyce Design; *b.* Joyce Design. 24: Joyce Design. 29: Grant Huntington for HMCo. 31: PhotoEdit. 32: *t.l.* Grant Huntington for HMCo.; *t.r.* Grant Huntington for HMCo. 33: *t.* Grant Huntington for HMCo.; *m.* Grant Huntington for HMCo.; *b.* Grant Huntington for HMCo. 35: *l.* Uniphoto Picture Agency; *r.* G.K. & Vikki Hart/The Image Bank. 37: David Phillips for HMCo. 38: *t.l.* The Image Bank; *t.r.* Bob Krist/Tony Stone Images. 39: *t.l.* Joe Cornish/Tony Stone Images; *t.r.* Phill Degginger/Color-Pic, Inc.; *b.* Superstock. 48: *l.* Richard Hutchings for HMCo.; *r.* Isaac Geib/Grant Heilman Photography, Inc. 50: *t.* Barry L. Runk/Grant Heilman Photography, Inc. 50–51: John Shaw/Tom Stack & Associates. 51: *b.* Climb High. 54: *t.* Richard Hutchings for HMCo. 55: *t.* Arthur D'Arazien/The Image Bank. 56: *t.* David R. Frazier Photography. 58–59: *bkgd.* Paul Trummer/The Image Bank; *inset* Michael Hampshirengs/National Geographic Society Image Collection.

Unit D 1: John M. Roberts/The Stock Market. 2–3: John M. Roberts/The Stock Market. 4–5: *bkgd.* Bruno P. Zehnder/Peter Arnold, Inc.; *inset* Corazon Claudio. 6: Elliott Smith for HMCo. 8: Frank Rossotto/The Stock Market. 9: *t.l.* Boyd Norton Worldwide Stock Photographs; *b.l.* Steve Wilkings/The Stock Market; *r.* E.R. Degginger/Color-Pic, Inc. 10: Larry Lefever/Grant Heilman Photography, Inc. 17: *l.* © John Meehan/Photo Researchers, Inc.; *r.* © Kent & Donna Dennen/Photo Researchers, Inc. 18: © Dingo Agence Vandystadt/Photo Researchers, Inc. 20: Chris Cone for HMCo. 20–21: John David Fleck/The Gamma Liaison Network. 21: © David M. Grossman/Photo Researchers, Inc. 27: *t.l.* Jeff Smith/The Image Bank; *t.r.* © 2000 Jim Richardson/Woodfin Camp & Associates; *b.l.* Lawrence Migdale Photography; *b.r.* Comstock. 36: Ken Karp for HMCo. 37: *t.l.* E.R. Degginger/Color-Pic, Inc.; *t.r.* © London School of Hygiene and Tropical Medicine/Science Photo Library/Photo Researchers, Inc.; *m.* © Moredon Animal Health, Ltd./Science Photo Library/Photo Researchers, Inc.; *b.l.* Brian Parker/Tom Stack & Associates; *b.r.* © Moredon Animal Health, Ltd./Science Photo Library/Photo Researchers, Inc. 46–47: *bkgd.* PhotoDisc, Inc; *inset* Richard Nowitz Photography. 51: *l.* © Francois Gohier/Photo Researchers, Inc.; *r.* David Stoecklein/The Stock Market. 52: © Douglas Faulkner/Photo Researchers, Inc. 53: © 2000 Leo Touchet/Woodfin Camp & Associates. 56: *t.* E.R. Degginger/Color-Pic, Inc.; *b.* © 2000 William Hubbell/Woodfin Camp & Associates. 56–58: *border* © 2000 Mike Yamashita/Woodfin Camp & Associates. 57: *t.l.* © 2000 G. Fokkema/Woodfin Camp & Associates; *t.m.* Tom Stack for HMCo.; *t.r.* E.R. Degginger/Color-Pic, Inc. 59: © 2000 Robert Frerck/Woodfin Camp & Associates. 60: *t.l.* The Stock Market; *t.r.* © 2000 Robert Frerck/Woodfin Camp & Associates; *b.l.* Carlos Humberto/The Stock Market; *b.r.* Dilip Mehta/The Stock Market. 61: © 2000 Robert Frerck/Woodfin Camp & Associates.